NORWAY

CAPPELEN DAMM

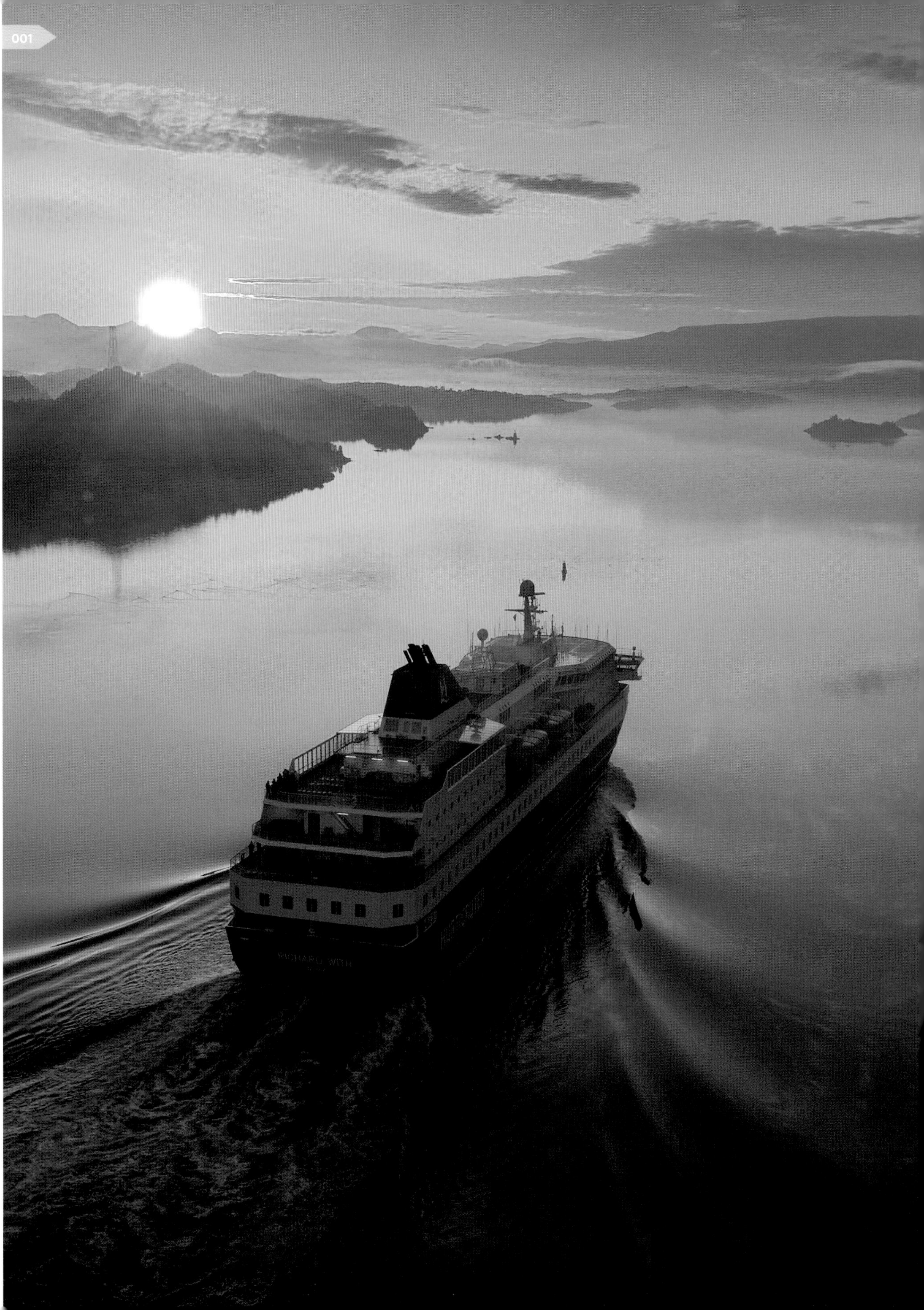

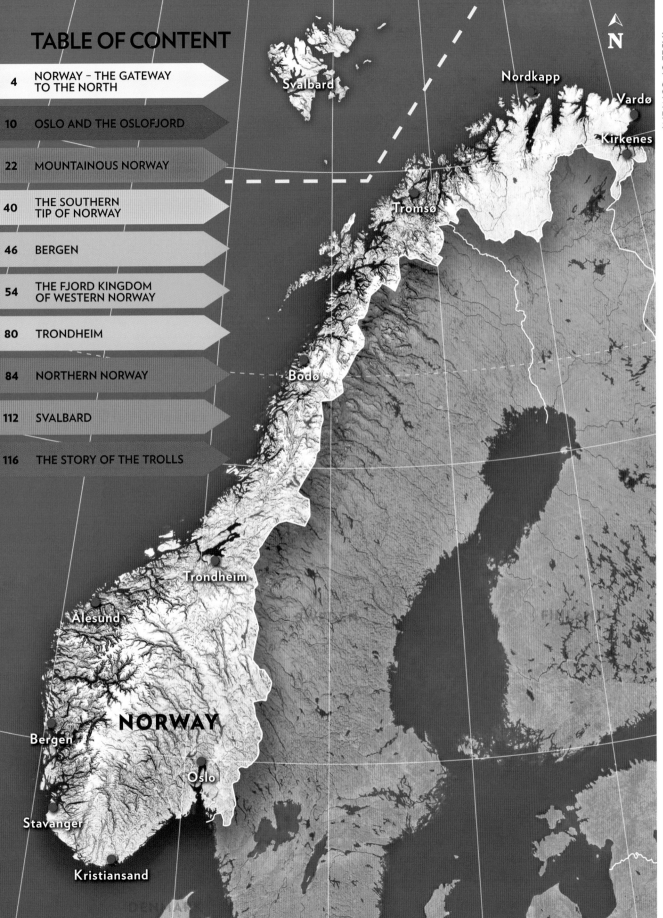

TABLE OF CONTENT

Svalbard

Nordkapp

Vardø

Kirkenes

Tromsø

Bodø

Trondheim

Ålesund

NORWAY

Bergen

Oslo

Stavanger

Kristiansand

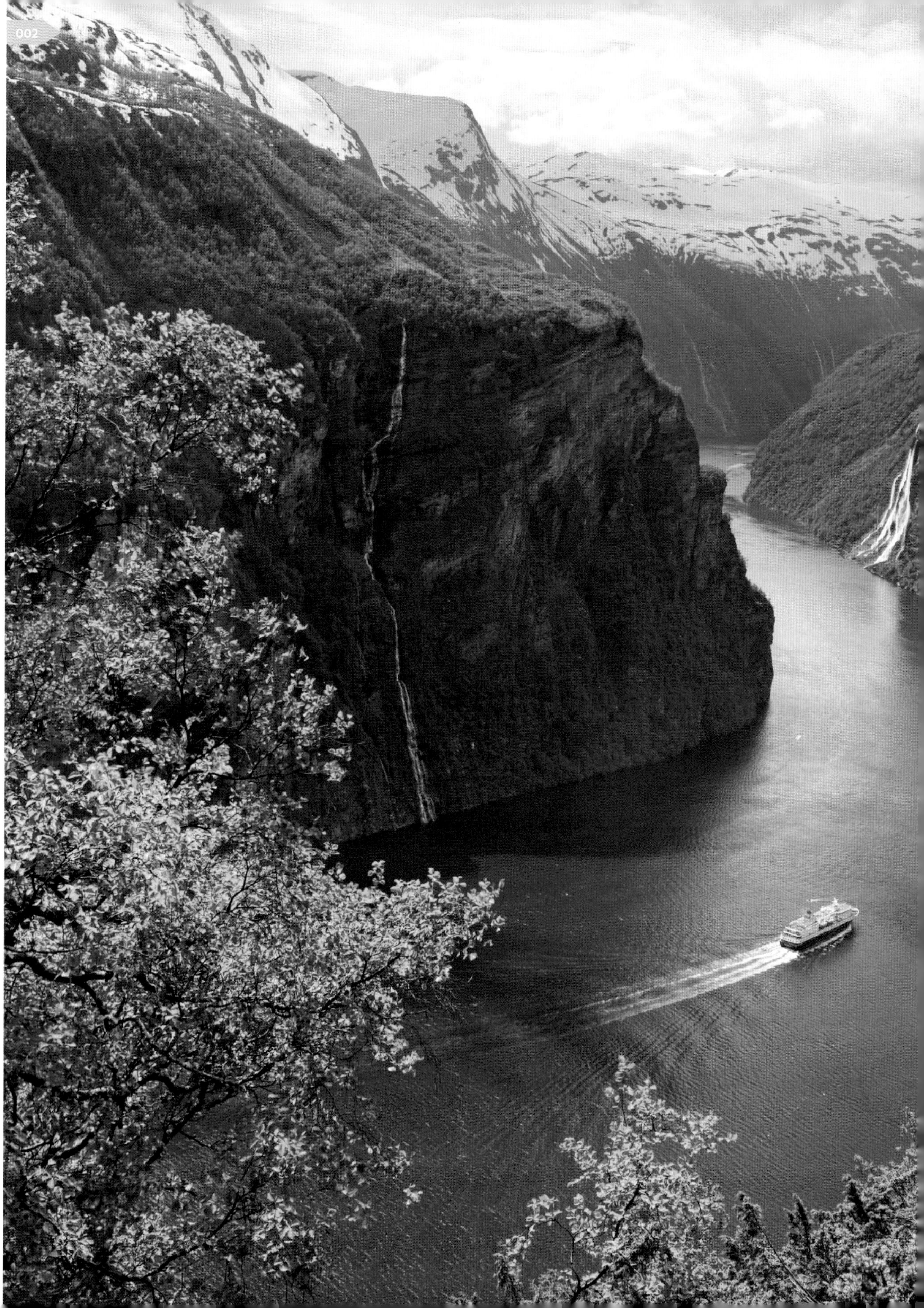

NORWAY – THE GATEWAY TO THE NORTH

The name 'Norway' means 'the gateway to the north'. If you travel from south to north you will experience a vast array of landscapes, culture and history. You will find fjords, mountains and waterfalls, large and small islands (scattered through the rough sea) between the mainland and harsh sea, national parks with untamed nature and glaciers, the midnight sun and northern lights, and towns, cities and villages that offer history and innovative culture. Have a wonderful journey!

To the east, Norway borders Russia, Finland and Sweden, and to the west the Atlantic Ocean. With its fjords, Norway's coastline stretches more than 20,000 kilometres. There are 2518 kilometres from the country's southernmost point (Lindesnes) to the northernmost point (the North Cape). Svalbard, Bjørnøya and Jan Mayen Island also belong to Norway.

Most of the population lives in Southern Norway in the most densely populated areas around Oslo, which is the capital city. The warm sea current from the Gulf of Mexico, called the Gulf Stream, allows people to inhabit latitudes that are uninhabitable in other parts of the world.

Dramatic nature

Norway has a vast variety of nature – both summer and winter. If you leave the coast while the climate is mild and head towards the middle of the country, you will quickly meet high mountains with harsh weather conditions.

The coast is broken up with small branches of fjords that stretch up to 200 kilometres inside the country. These narrows fjords with mountains that rise steeply from the water to more than 1000 metres above sea level are among the most popular tourist attractions in Norway.

The landscape of eastern and central Norway is quite flat, while Northern Norway offers stunning and rugged nature. Here, the midnight sun shines 24 hours a day in the summer, while in the winter darkness prevails and there is hardly a ray of light at midday.

Norway – before and now

Human beings have inhabited Norway as it is known today for more than 10,000 years. For thousands of years Norwegians survived by hunting, fishing and farming.

The fabled Vikings ruled for 300 years from approximately 800 AD, known for their rampages in other countries. Just before 900 AD King Harald Hårfagre united Norway as one kingdom. A hundred years later, King Olav Tryggvason and King Olav the Holy introduced Christianity to the country.

Norway was greatly affected by the Black Death during 1348–1350 when at least half of the population died. In 1537 the so-called '400-year-night' started. This was when Norway was controlled by Denmark through its union with the country.

Norway received its first constitution in 1814, and in 1905 the country became

001   Hurtigruten sails northwards under the midnight sun.
002   A cruise ship enters Geirangerfjord, one of the most famous and visited fjords in Western Norway.
003   The Norwegian coastal landscape is dramatic in many places with steep mountains that dive into the sea. From Værøy in Lofoten.
004   Winter in Jotunheimen.
005   The 17th of May is celebrated across the country with children's parades and corps music. This children's parade in Oslo winds its way up Karl Johans Gate to the palace to greet the Royal Family.
006   King Harald V, Queen Sonja, Crown Prince Haakon Magnus, Crown Princess Mette-Marit and Princess Ingrid Alexandra.

005

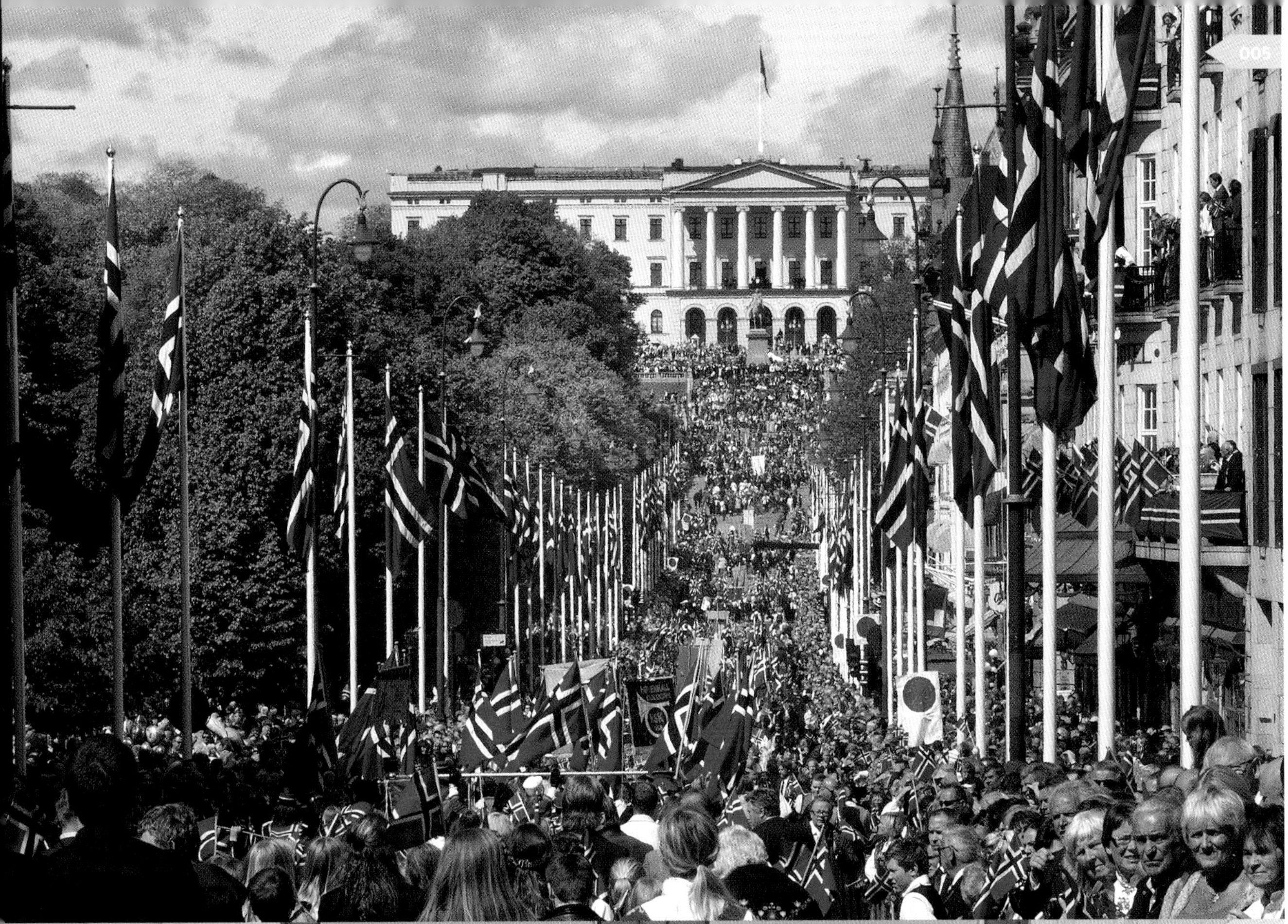

006

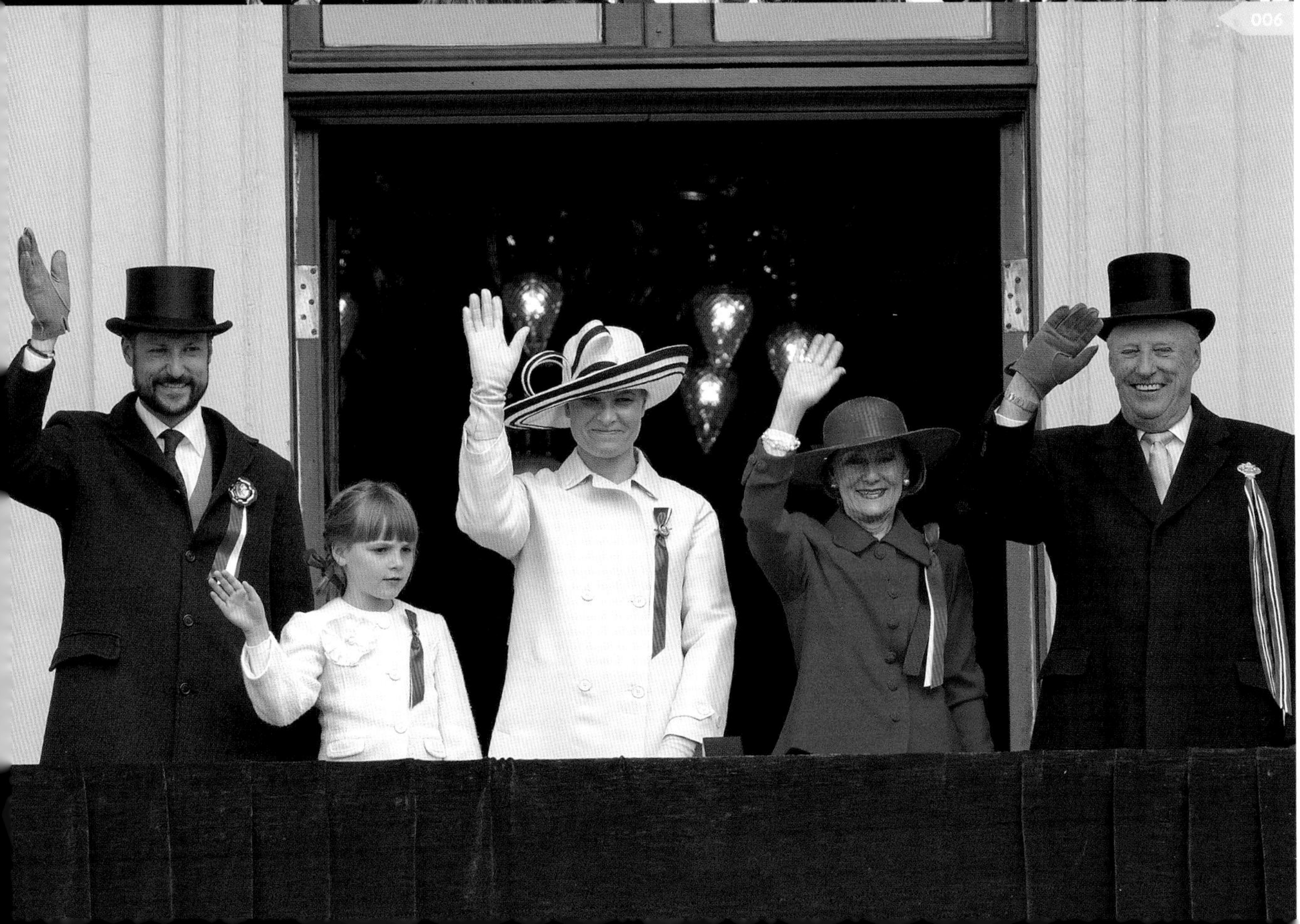

independent. Since then, Norway has had three kings: King Haakon VII, King Olav V and King Harald V.

Norway is a constitutional monarchy. The King is the head of state, but has no official political power. The country is led according to parliamentary principles, in which the Norwegian Parliament (Storting) has legislative power and the Government executive power. Through two referendums in 1972 and 1994 respectively, Norway elected not to become a member of the European Union (EU).

Norway has become a world leader when it comes to building up the modern welfare state, which aims to create social and financial security for its citizens. This means complex state benefit and pensions schemes, free health services, good support schemes for families with children, in addition to free education for all.

Since the 1970s oil and gas have been extracted from the Norwegian Continental Shelf. Today Norway is one of the leading exporters of oil and one of the main suppliers of gas to the European continent. Norway is also the fourth largest shipping nation in the world, in addition to a large exporter of fish.

The fisheries have been a crucial industry since the Middle Ages.

Culture

Norway has a rich and vibrant culture, and several artists have been recognised abroad. Among them, dramatist Henrik Ibsen (1828–1906), who is one of the most renowned. His famous dramas, for example 'A Doll's House' and 'Ghosts' are often staged in the world's most important theatres.

Three Norwegian writers have received the Nobel Prize for literature: Bjørnstjerne

007

008

Bjørnson (1832–1910) received the price in 1903. He wrote novels, poems and plays, in addition to the Norwegian national anthem 'Ja, vi elsker'.

The very productive writer Knut Hamsun (1859–1952) received the Nobel Prize in 1920 for his novel 'The Growth of the Soil', while Sigrid Undset (1882–1949) received the prize eight years later. She wrote many novels, which are set in Norway in the Middle Ages.

Not only have Norwegians been recognised for literature, but also other aspects of culture. Edvard Munch (1863–1944) became world famous with his painting 'The Scream'. Edvard Grieg (1843–1970) is Norway's greatest classical music composer. 'In the Hall of the Mountain King' is one of his many well-known pieces.

Opera singer Kirsten Flagstad (1895–1962) belongs among the top soprano singers of all times and is one of the most internationally celebrated Norwegian women.

Norwegians have also been recognised in modern times. Actress and Director Liv Ullman has become famous partly due to her involvement in the films of Swedish Ingmar Bergman, while the pop group A-ha has toured the world during the last decade.

Norwegians who are involved in culture find success abroad within all areas of culture, which contributes to boosting Norway's position on the world map.

007 Along some parts of the coast one can get a glimpse of the lights from the oil platforms far out in the North Sea.

008 Dried fish, mainly cod, is dried on racks or in a separate drying facility. Dried fish is the product that Norway has exported the longest. A more recent export product is farmed fish, particularly salmon.

009 'The Scream' (painted in 1893) is Edvard Munch's most famous painting.

010 Henrik Ibsen is one of Norway's most famous writers. His plays are continually staged in theatres worldwide.

OSLO AND THE OSLOFJORD

The capital of Norway is surrounded by beautiful nature innermost on Norway's fifth longest fjord. If you come by sea you will experience the most beautiful gateway you could ever wish for. After passing the idyllic skerries of Oslofjord, you are welcomed by the architectonic pearl, the Oslo Opera House, situated in Oslo's newest neighbourhood.

Oslo's location is unique. The centre of the city points directly towards the fjord.

It is encircled by extensive forests, and mountains lie within close range. Norwegians love nature, and in Oslo a boat trip on the fjord, a walk, bicycle ride or a skiing trip in Nordmarka is always available nearby. A short ferry trip to the small islands in the fjord (or an equally short trip by metro to Nordmarka) takes you far away from busy city life.

Oslo was made the capital of Norway as early as in the mid 11th century by King Harald Hardråde. A great fire in 1624 destroyed many of the old buildings, however the city was moved and quickly rebuilt by Danish King Christian IV, and it was named Christiania. Three hundred years later the city was re-named Oslo.

Today, with approximately 633,000 inhabitants, Oslo is a modern city with numerous attractions; for example, landmarks such as the Oslo Opera House, the Oslo City Hall and the recently built ski jumping hill Holmenkollbakken.

In the Norwegian capital you can experience one of Norway's most visited tourist attractions, the unique Vigeland Sculpture Park with Gustav Vigeland's sculptures, or you can visit the Munch Museum and enjoy the vision of the paintings by one of Norway's most famous artists, Edvard Munch.

Not far from the centre you will find the rural Bygdøy Peninsula with Viking ships, Fridtjof Nansen's polar ship 'Fram', Thor Heyerdahl's Kon-Tiki raft and the Norwegian Museum of Cultural History, which houses all the old and traditional timber buildings typical of rural areas.

Oslo is continually changing. Around the new Opera House (where the city has its waterline) a new and contemporary suburb is developing. This emphasises the city's close proximity to the fjord.

Along the Oslofjord new experiences are awaiting you. On the east side lie the white painted summer towns of Drøbak and Son, Fredrikstad with its cosy old town and the mighty Fredriksten Fortress in Halden. On the west side of the fjord is the Slottsfjell Mountain in Norway's oldest city, Tønsberg, Edvard Munch's Åsgårdstrand and Blaafarveverket at Modum are places you should visit.

012

013

011   Karl Johans Gate, which leads up to the palace, is the main street of Oslo.

012   From the Holmenkollbakken ski jumping hill located in the hills above Oslo you have a wonderful view of the fjord and city, which is blanketed in its winter glory here.

013   Oslo City Hall looms like a monument with its two massive towers measuring 63 and 66 metres respectively. The Town Hall Square extends down to the water and towards Aker Brygge, which buzzes with life during summer.

014   Oslo seen from the seaside.

015   The Royal Palace with a statue of King Karl Johan in the background lies at the top of Oslo's main street, Karl Johans Gate.

018

019

016 The Oslo Opera House has a beautiful location by the edge of the fjord. It became the city's new landmark after it was opened in 2008.

017 The Storting, the Norwegian Parliament House, is situated on Karl Johans Gate in the middle of Oslo City Centre.

018 Oslo's magnificent castle from the Middle Ages, Akershus Fortress, has protected the city against intruders from the seaside since the 1300s.

019 The Oslo Opera House is the first opera house in the world with a roof you can walk on!

021

022

020 The Vigeland Sculpture Park is the world's first sculpture collection made by one person, Gustav Vigeland (1869–1943). The collection comprises 192 sculptures in all.

021 The park's sculptures represent people in all phases of life, and they awake the interest of both adults and children.

022 At the highest point of Vigeland Park stands the Monolith, a 17-metre high column that includes 121 human figures. The column is made of one piece of stone, hence the name 'Monolith'.

023 Sinnataggen, the Angry Little Boy, is one of the smallest sculptures in Vigeland Park, and also the most known.

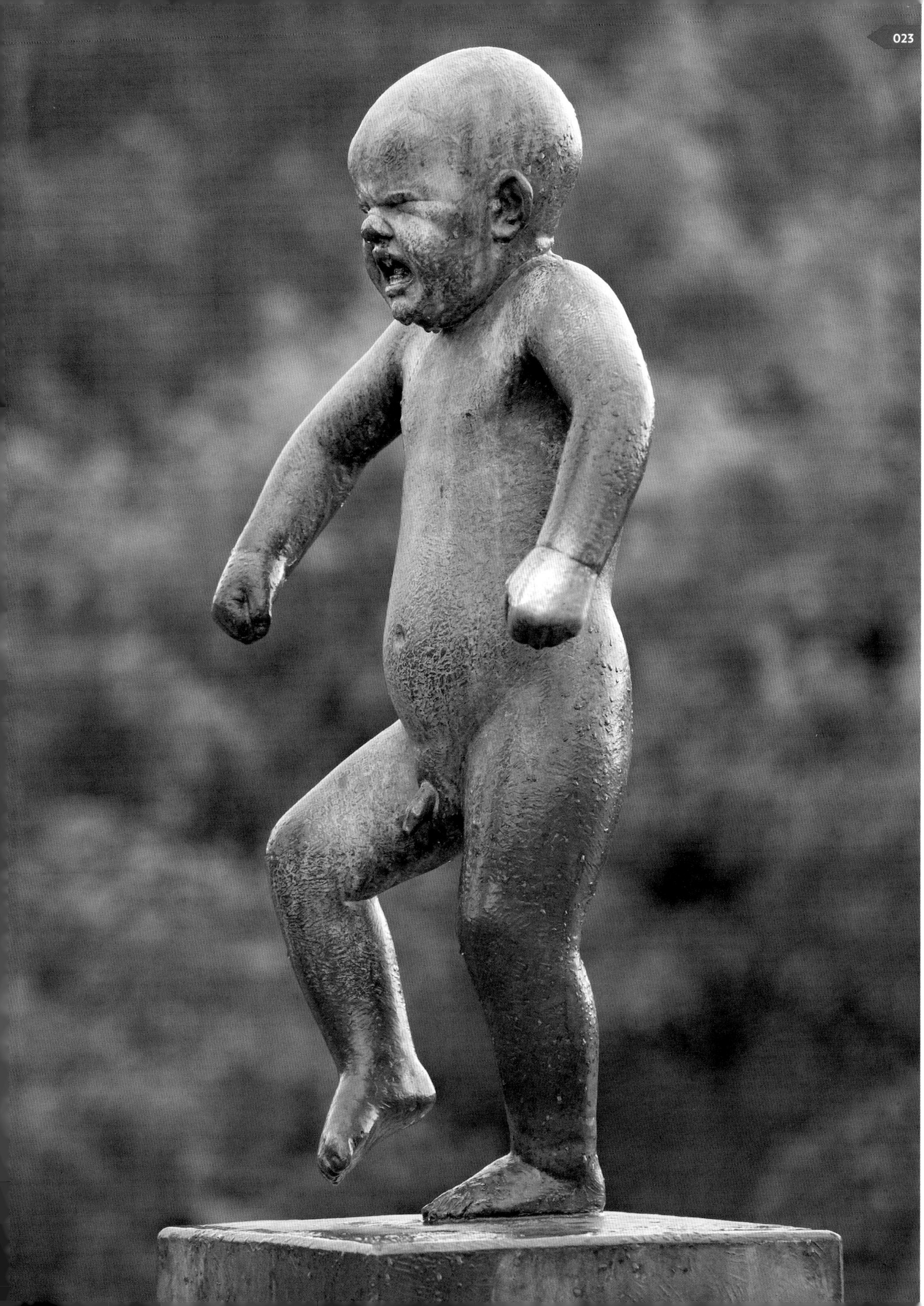

024 The Kon-Tiki Museum houses the original balsa raft Kon-Tiki, which carried the world famous discoverer Thor Heyerdahl (1914–2002) and his crew over the Pacific Ocean from Peru to Polynesia in 1947.

025 The Oseberg ship is one of three Viking ships from the 9th and 10th centuries, exhibited in the Viking Ship Museum.

026 The Norwegian Museum of Cultural History is Norway's largest cultural history museum. It is comprised of approximately 150 old houses collected from around the country and restored in this large park.

027 At Bygdøy stands the national monument for the first people to reach the South Pole. Roald Amundsen (in the centre) reached the South Pole in 1911 and his ship, 'Gjøa' is exhibited at the Norwegian Maritime Museum (seen in the background). Next to this is the Fram Museum. 'Fram'is the sailing ship that carried another Norwegian polar explorer, Fridtjof Nansen, towards the North Pole during 1893 to 1896. Nansen and his companion were the first in the world to reach the North Pole after a long and strenuous trip on skis.

028 Norwegian national costumes are found in many designs and it was created around the dissolution of the union in 1905. they are inspired by traditional folklore costumes.

029 In 2011 the World Ski Championships were arranged in Oslo. A large public festival was held in Nordmarka.

030 A well-deserved break during a skiing trip is expected at one of Nordmarka's restaurants.

031 Oslo is surrounded by beautiful nature and Nordmarka is a popular place for the city's inhabitants throughout the year. During the winter, cross-country skiing is the main activity.

032 Many fine beaches are found along Oslofjord.

033 On a lush island in Oslofjord lies the Oscarborg Fortress.

034 Oslofjord is frequently used by boat enthusiasts during the summer.

032

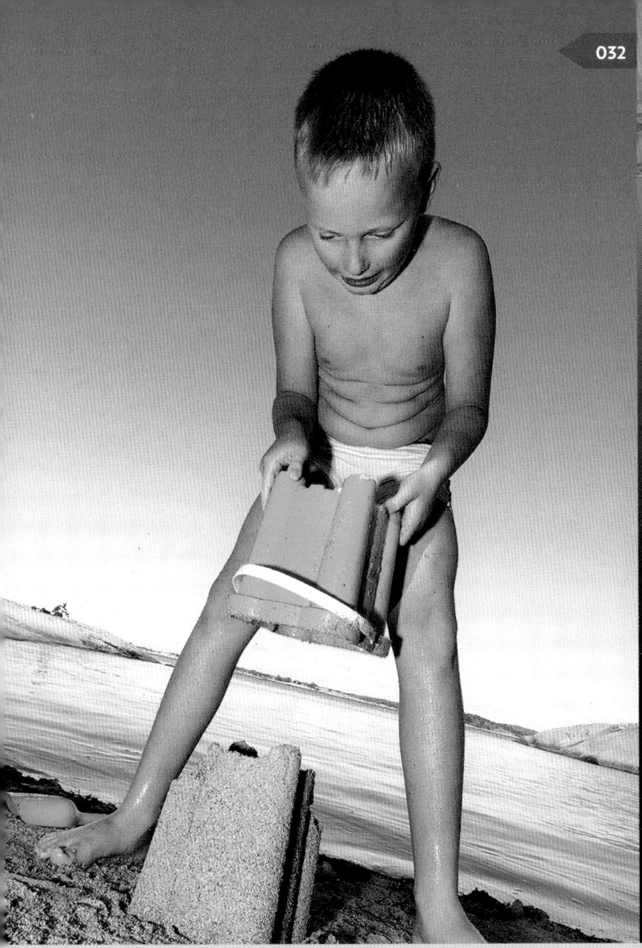

033

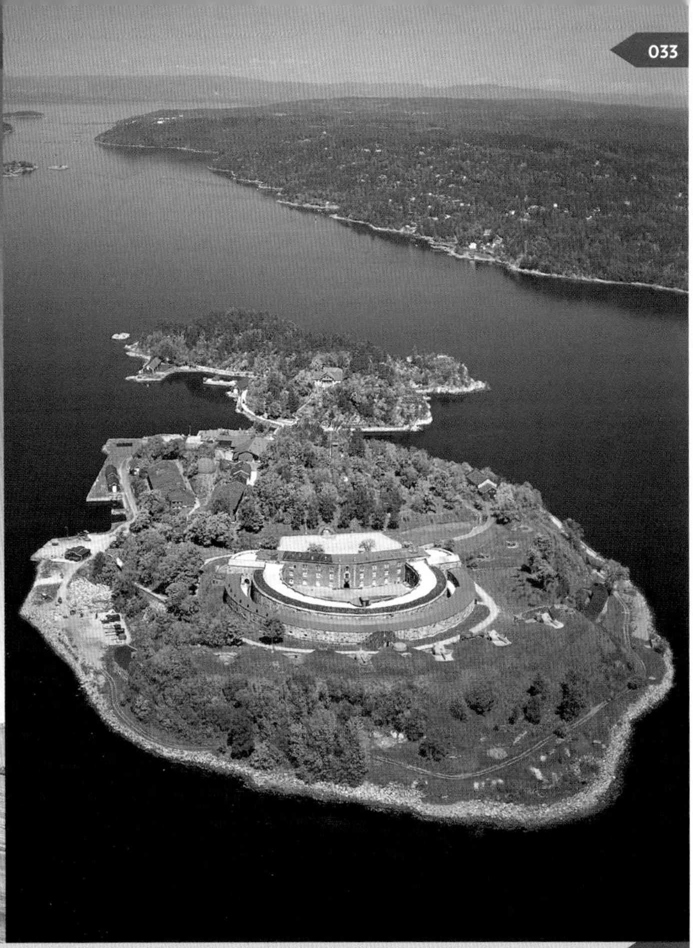

034

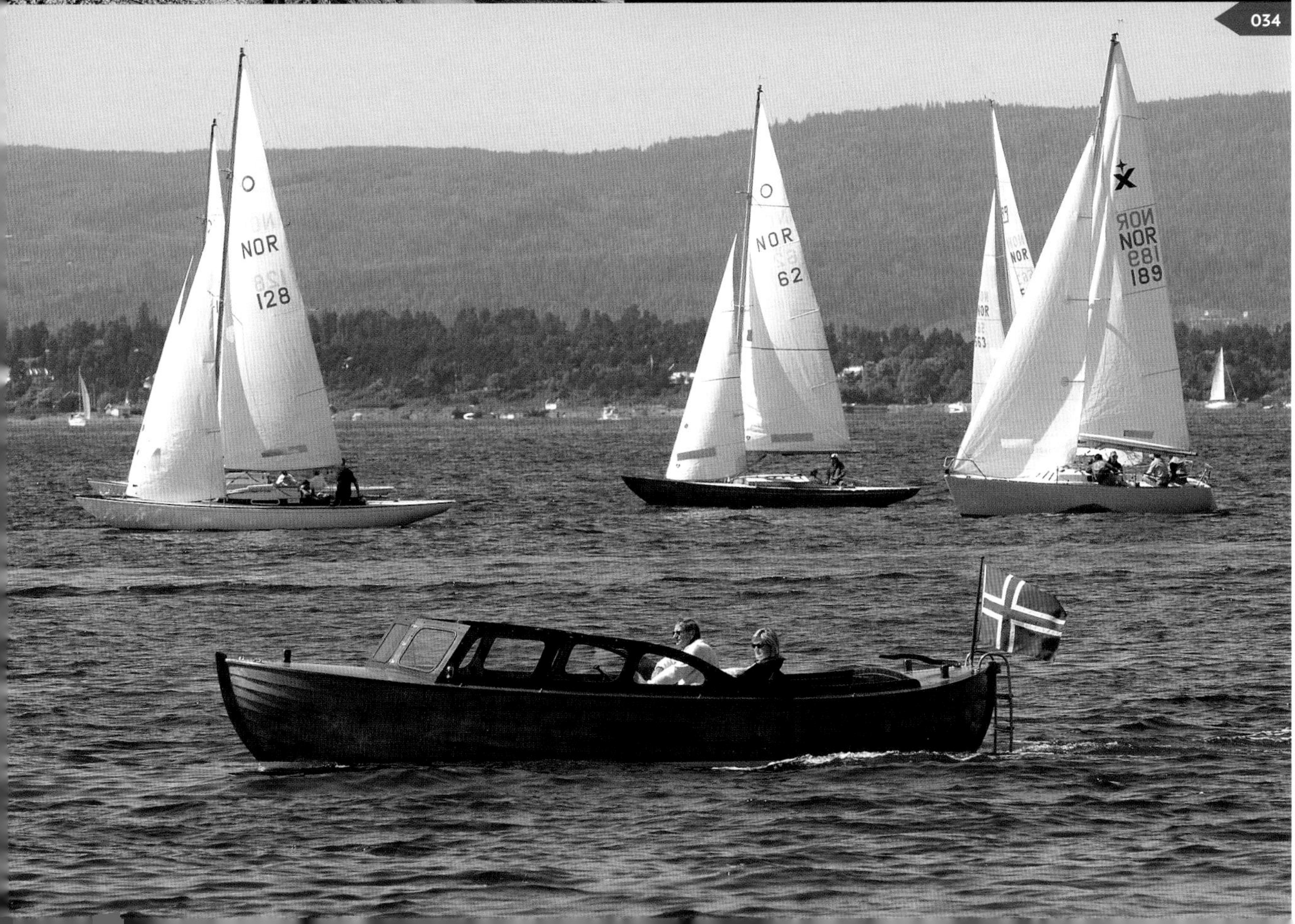

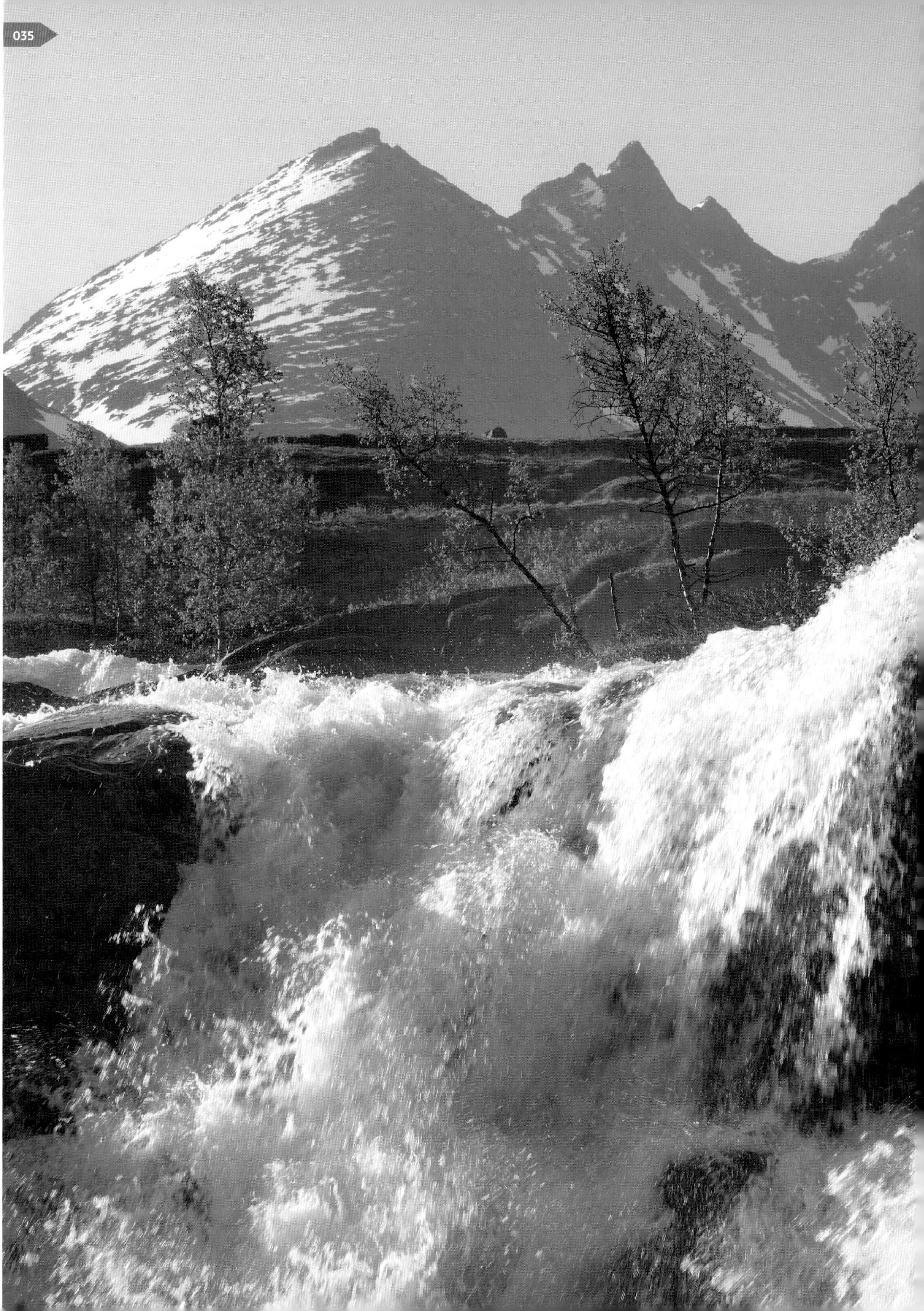

MOUNTAINOUS NORWAY – HOME OF THE TROLLS

The magnificent nature in Norway's mountainous areas is dramatic with high peaks, steep cliffs, endless plateaus, deep forests and lush valleys with wild rivers. Almost a third of Norway is comprised of mountains. Most of the mountains are found in the southern part of the country where they form a 'spine' between the numerous fjords that extend towards the sea to the west, and extensive forests and landscape of corn-yellow fields towards Sweden to the east. The trolls come from these mountains.

Norwegians have a close and active relationship with the untouched nature in mountain areas during the summer and winter alike.

In Jotunheimen you can go mountain climbing or rafting in the valley's arduous rivers. Or how about a skiing trip on the glaciers in the middle of the summer? Hiking along marked trails in the high mountains, on the open plateaus or in the tranquil forests are perfect if you are seeking peacefulness.

The Olympic 1994 towns: Lillehammer, Gjøvik and Hamar are situated around Norway's largest lake – Mjøsa. The towns provide a good starting point for getting to know the Norwegian mountain range, which includes Trollheimen, Dovrefjell and Rondane in the north, and the mighty Jotunheimen, as well as the wide-stretching Hardangervidda further south. The long and beautiful valleys in Hallingdal, Valdres, Gudbrandsdalen and Østerdalen lead you up to and inside the magnificent mountain range.

The mountains and valleys preserve many cultural treasures like the mining town of Røros with its unique timber constructions, and the characteristic stave churches in the valleys with their wonderful examples of Norwegian rose painting.

Norway's oldest paddle steamer, Skibladner, is in operation in Mjøsa during the summer and takes you to Lillehammer, Gjøvik and Hamar, where you can visit Hamar Cathedral, and other sights. In Lillehammer you can also allow yourself to be impressed by old Norwegian farm architecture at Maihaugen. Or how about a visit to Telemark, the cradle of skiing? From here you can experience an unusual sea voyage on the Telemark Canal, which takes you towards the sea through the endless skerries of southern Norway.

035 The view towards the Skagastølstindene peaks in Jotunheimen.

036 On a bicycle trip in Norwegian mountains.

037 Hamar Cathedral is listed for its ruins, which originate from the old cathedral from approximately 1200 AD. The cathedral ruins were enclosed in glass in 1998 to protect them from frost damage and moisture.

038 Skibladner from 1856 is Norway's only paddle steamer. It is still in operation on Norway's largest lake.

039 The Maihaugen Museum comprises an impressive collection of old buildings collected from Lillehammer or nearby valleys.

040 A rope team crosses a glacier on the route from Galdhøpiggen,
Norway's highest mountain (2469 metres above seal level).

041 Gjendinebua in Jotunheimen.

042 Autumn in Jotunheimen.

043 1994 was the year Norway arranged the Olympics in
Lillehammer. This is from the closing ceremony.

044 Besseggen in Jotunheimen.

045 Jotunheimen in its winter costume. This is Norway's wildest
mountain range with most of the highest mountain peaks in
Norway. The mountains tower 2000 metres above sea level.

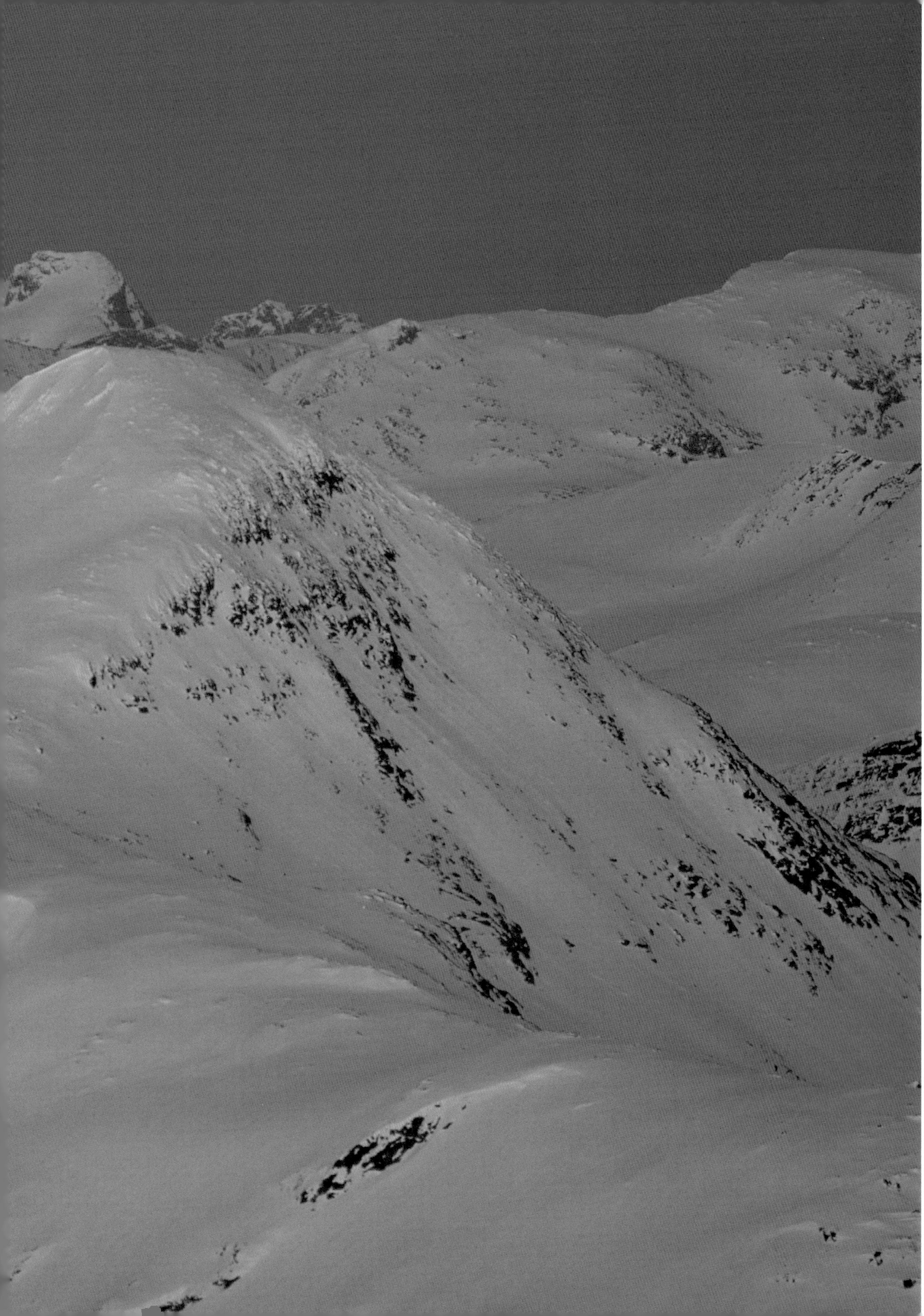

046   Autumn cascades across Rondane.
047   Goats are a permanent sight in the mountains. The special
         Norwegian goat cheese is made by turning goat's milk into
         cheese.
048   Wild, free roaming reindeer in Tynset.
049   At the entrance to Trollheimen.
050   In the untouched wilderness on Dovrefjell Mountain you can
         go on a musk ox safari.

052

051 Røros Church with its characteristic tower is situated in the centre of the town.

052 The tradition rich Rørosmartnan Winter Festival has been arranged every year since 1854 and it lasts for five days.

053 Røros lies 600 metres above sea level. The foundation of the Røros community was the mining company, Røros Copper Works. The town is therefore called Bergstaden (the mining town). Many significant cultural monuments are found in the area, and the whole of Bergstaden is on UNESCO'S World Cultural Heritage List.

054 Gaustatoppen lies 1883 metres above sea level and boasts one of the best views in the country. On a clear day you can see more than one sixth of the area of mainland Norway.

055 Girls in the Hallingdal national costume.
056 Beautiful silver jewellery are necessary accessories for the national costumes.
057 Wood carving is a traditional art handicraft in Norway. Here you can see animal ornaments, which form part of the decorations in Heddal stave church.
058 Norwegian rose painted interior in Heddal stave church.
059 In the Middle Ages approximately one thousand stave churches were erected in Norway. Today only 28 of these impressive and completely distinctive timber churches remain. Heddal stave church in Telemark is the largest of them all.

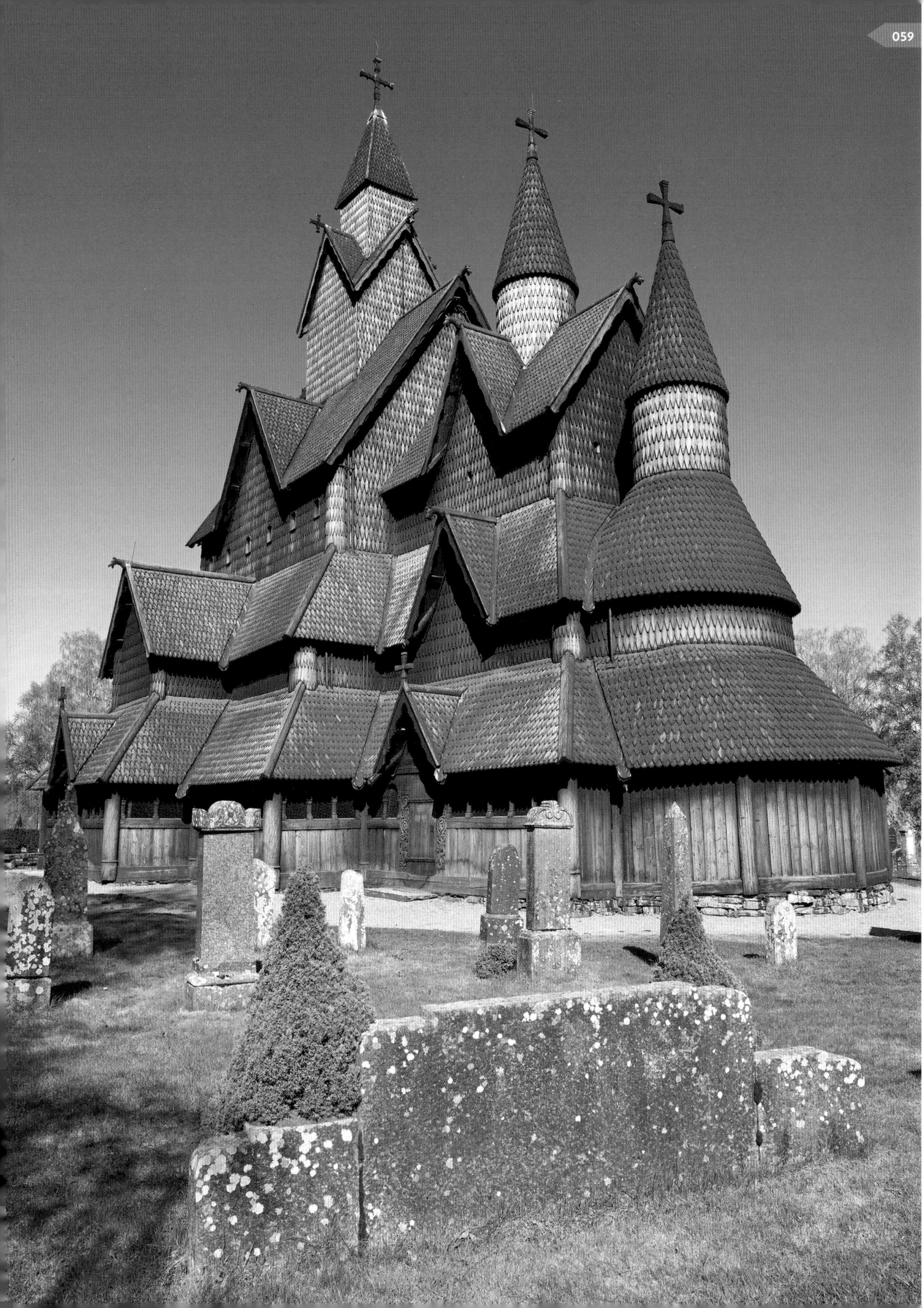

060 Rafting in the wild Sjoa River that runs down the mountains.

061 Elk in the vast forests of Femunden.

062 A ski jumper swaying freely in Morgedal in Telemark, the home of Sondre Norheim. He was a great pioneer in the development of modern skiing as a sport.

063 Hardangervidda is Northern Europe's highest mountain plateau and is the largest of Norway's many national parks.

064 500 men spent five years blasting the Telemark Canal, which extends from the foot of Hardangervidda right down towards the coast to the town of Skien. The canal was completed in 1892 and at that time it was one of the most impressive pieces of engineering in the world.

063

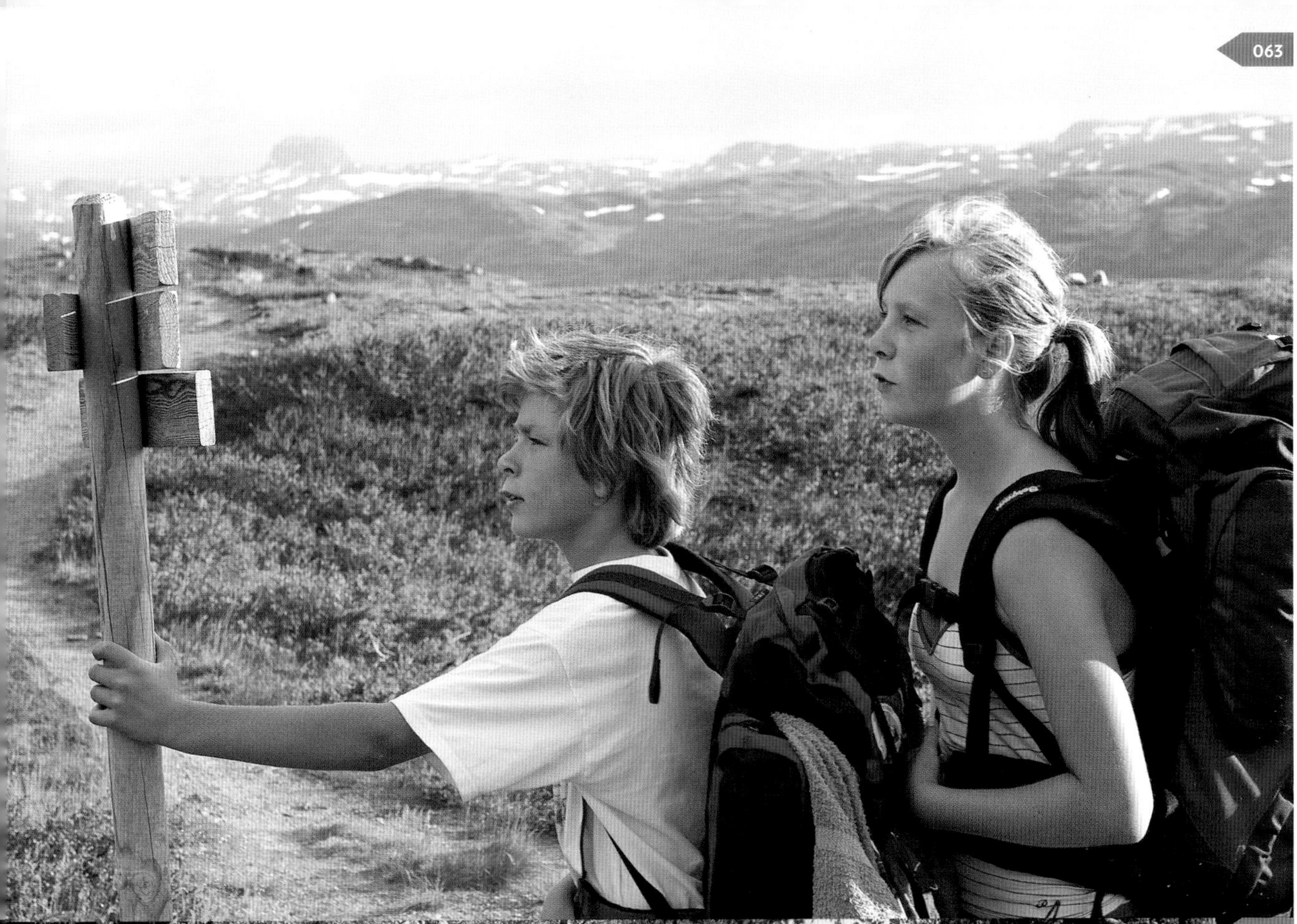

064

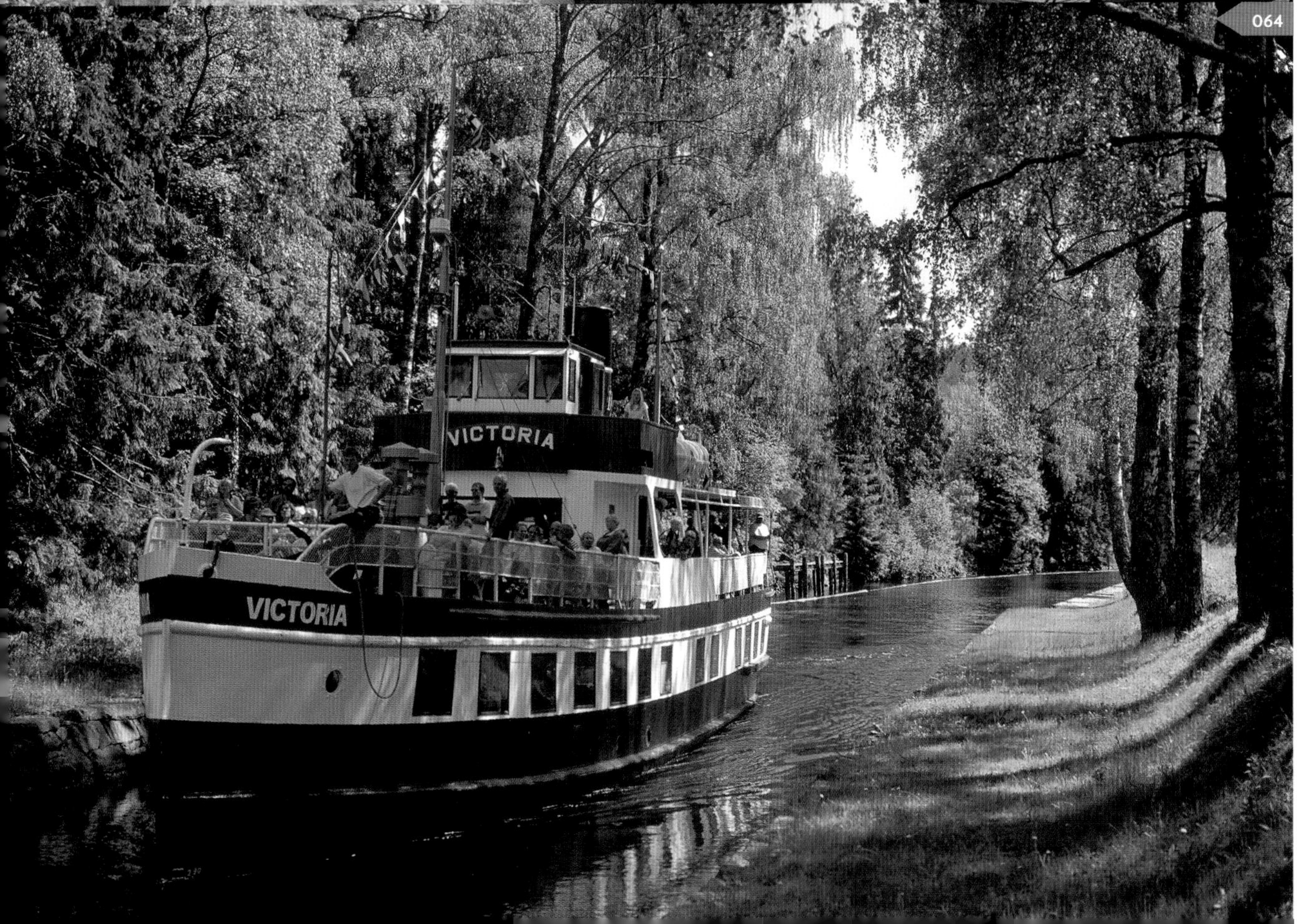

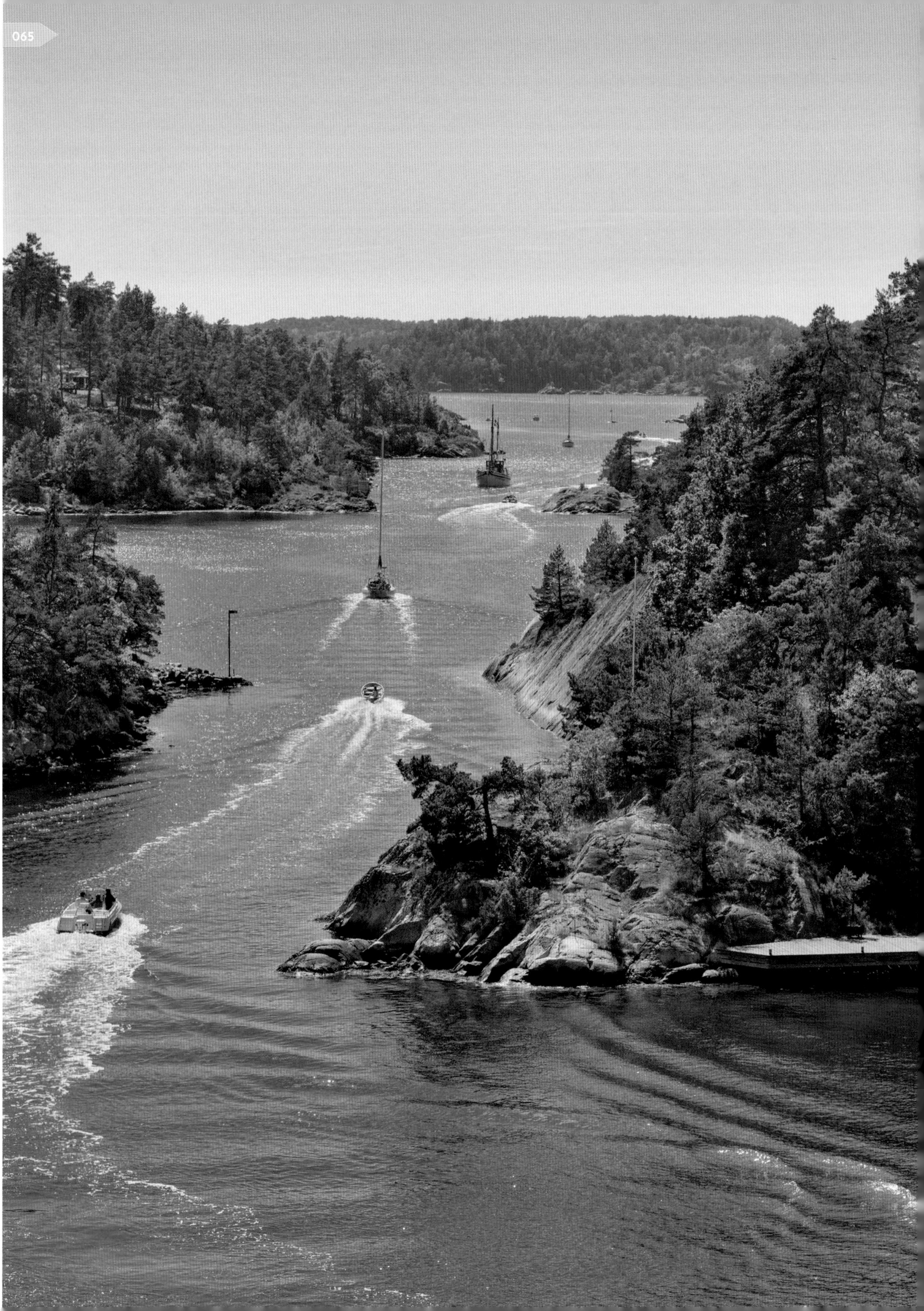

THE SOUTHERN TIP OF NORWAY

The beautiful coastline from Skien where the Telemark Canal merges and westwards to Stavanger constitutes the southern tip of Norway. Here you will the find perfect idyllicness of the Norwegian holiday landscape – charming villages with white painted timber houses and vibrant harbours, warm rocks and hoarse seagull screams, salty sea and droning wooden boats. For many Norwegians, warm and sunny days in the southern achipelago is the definition of a summer holiday.

Risør, Grimstad and Lillesand are among the many pearls along the southern coast of Norway, and people come here throughout the summer to experience wooden boat festivals, culture arrangements and lazy days in their cabins. Throughout the ages, artists have allowed themselves to be inspired by the idyllic villages of southern Norway and the coastal landscape. The world renowned painter Edvard Munch was one of these.

The numerous harbour towns along the southern coast of Norway flourished during the era of the great sailing ships in the 1800s, due to abundant activity in shipping, fishing and trading. Traces of this golden age are found in the beautiful patrician houses belonging to local shipping companies and tradesmen, and it can also be seen in the large trading houses.

Kristiansand is the largest city in southern Norway. It was founded by Christian IV as a fortress city in 1642. Just west of Kristiansand is Mandal, which is Norway's most southern town, and if you continue a bit further to the west, you will reach Norway's most southern point, Lindesnes. From here it is 2518 kilometres to Norway's most northern point, the North Cape.

Before you reach Stavanger, the stunning coastal lowland area of Jæren extends down to the harsh sea. Orrestranden is also found here, which is Norway's longest sandy beach. Within the boundaries of the endless sandy beaches, some of Norway's most fertile agricultural areas is found.

Stavanger is the fourth largest city in Norway and has been nick-named the Oil City since it is the centre of the Norwegian offshore oil industry.

The white painted and cosy old town lies around Vågen and should be experienced before you embark on an excursion down the magnificent Norwegian fjords.

065   Blindleia is an idyllic inland waterway between Lillesand on the mainland and the surrounding islands.

066   The massive potholes outside Risør are some of largest in Northern Europe. Earlier it was thought that trolls used them to make food, but today they are used for bathing.

067   View over Norway's most southern town, Mandal, with the gateway and open sea beyond.

068   Brekkestø is the pure symbol of the summery idyllicness of Southern Norway.

069   A Colin Archer boat outside Risør. Colin Archer was Norway's most prominent boat constructor at the end of the 1800s. He developed new types of boats that withstood bad weather and difficult sailing conditions.

070 The national monument 'Sword in the Mountain' was erected
to commemorate the Battle of Hafrsfjord in the 9th Century
– one of the largest and most important battles during Viking
times when Norway's first king, Harald Hårfagre, beat the local
small kings and united Norway as one kingdom.

071 The cosy old town of Norway's fourth largest city, Stavanger
(approximately 130,000 inhabitants) lies in a cliff down
towards the harbour.

072 Norway's oldest lighthouse lies in Lindesnes. For a long time it
was an important landmark for all shipping traffic to and from
the Baltic Sea.

073 A sign that quantifies Norway as a long stretching country.

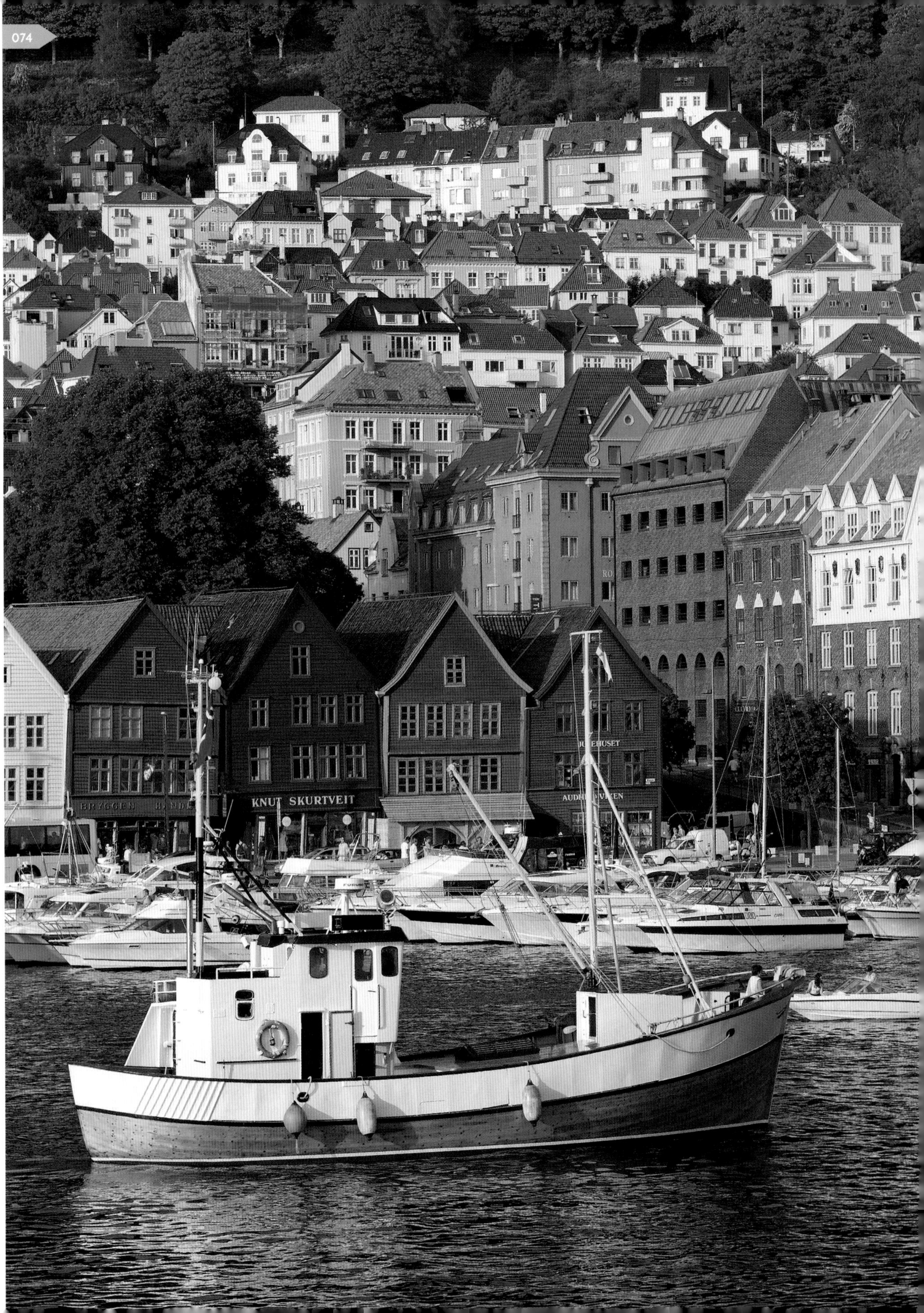
BRYGGEN
KNUT SKURTVEIT

BERGEN – THE FJORD CAPITAL OF WESTERN NORWAY

Bergen is situated by the sea on the west of Norway and is surrounded by seven high mountains. The city is a charming mix of characteristic timber houses with roots dating back to Hanseatic times. Lively crowds along the harbour, innovative trading through enterprises and stalls, and not to mention an inviting fishing market. Take the funicular up the mountain to experience a fantastic view over the city below your feet.

Bergen with more than 270,000 inhabitants is often called the capital of Western Norway and is Norway's second largest city. The city is a popular tourist attraction and a natural starting point for trips to the country's famous fjords.

Therefore, Bergen is also among Europe's most sought-after ports of call for cruise ships.

The city was founded in 1070 by Olav Kyrre under the name of Bjørgvin, which means 'the green meadow between the mountains'.

For a while during the Middle Ages Bergen was Scandinavia's largest city and a trading and shipping city of European importance.

For centuries the city had a monopoly on the export of fish caught between Western Norway and Finnmark.

During the 13th and 14th centuries, the Hanseatic League had one of its four most central foreign trading stations in Bergen and it controlled most of the trading along the Wharf. Today the old and characteristic trading houses from Hanseatic times represent the city, and they have been included on UNESCO's World Heritage List.

Throughout its history Bergen has had 36 great city fires. The biggest was in 1702 when 90 percent of the city and the whole of Bryggen Wharf was just ashes.

In the years that followed, Bryggen was restored to its original design.

Bergen continues to be an important trading and shipping city with Norway's second largest port. Its location between the coast and city mountains means that it 'always' rains in Bergen. Approximately three times as much rain falls here as it does in Oslo.

Bergen is also the starting point for the 'world's most beautiful coastal voyage', that is, Hurtigruten's five-and-a-half-day excursion to Kirkenes far in the north of Norway. The ship has carried passengers, cargo and mail through the stunning Norwegian nature – on spectacular fjords towards the midnight sun or under the northern lights and along the rough coast of Northern Norway.

074 Bergen's timber house development seen from Vågen.

075 A walk between the Bryggen Wharf's old Hanseatic timber buildings. The buildings originally stem from the Middle Ages and are one of the most popular tourist attractions in Norway. The timber development is comprised of 61 preserved buildings, which are also on UNESCO's World Cultural Heritage List.

076 At the famous fishing market at the end of Vågen, you can taste and purchase most of the creatures that move in the sea.

077 Bryggen's characteristic building facades.

078 Bergen.

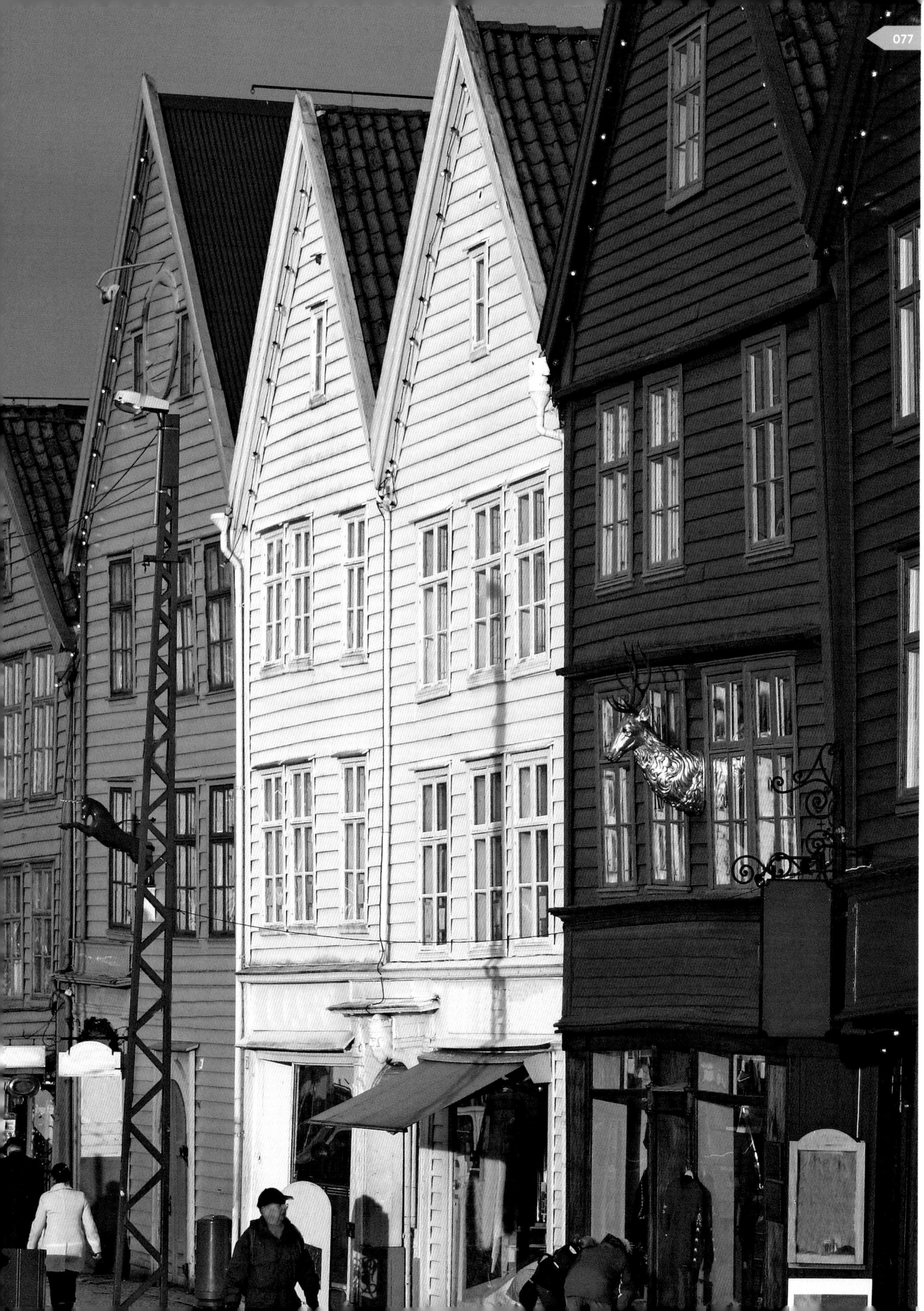

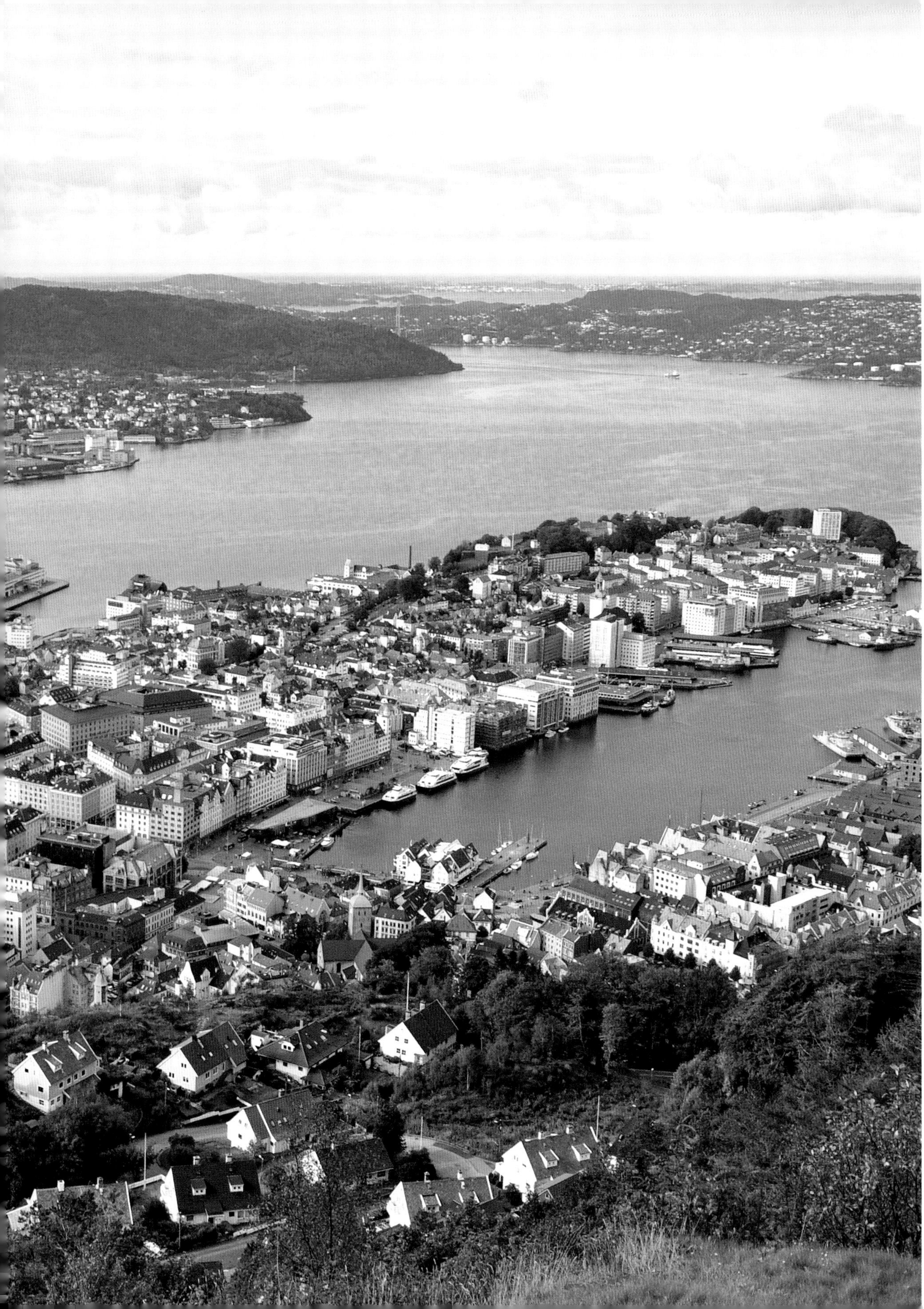

079 A fantastic view of Bergen is seen from Mount Fløien. Hop on the funicular from the fish market and it will take you to the final stop on Mount Fløien, which lies 320 metres above sea level.

080 The Ulriksbanen cable car takes only three minutes from Bergen City Centre up to Ulriken Mountain, which lies 642 metres above sea level. Here you can go for a hike in the large and nature rich area, or just enjoy the view.

081 Troldhaugen is the home of composer Edvard Grieg. The house was built in 1885 and is now a museum. If you go inside the villa, you will see Grieg's Steinway grand piano from 1892, which continues to be used for concerts.

082 The Bergen Aquarium is Norway's oldest and largest aquarium with seals, penguins and fish species from seas near and far. Approximately 250,000 people annually visit the aquarium to witness the spectacular feeding of the seals and penguins.

083 Edvard Grieg named the house Troldhaugen 'my best opus number so far', even though it was drawn by his male cousin.

THE FJORD KINGDOM OF WESTERN NORWAY

Norway's mountains are not the highest in the world, it only looks like they are. From a boat, inwards on a fjord, you see them plunge steeply down into turquoise blue water, while the waterfalls cascade down the mountain face. In the Norwegian fjord kingdom, you can experience overwhelming nature, which is both idyllic and dramatic simultaneously.

The Norwegian word 'fjord' has not become internationally known for nothing: the long stretching Norwegian coastline is one of the areas in the world that has the most fjords – almost 1200 fjords have been given their own name. Some of these are also among the longest in the world, for example, Sognefjord (204 km) and Hardangerfjord (180 km). These are found in the western part of the country between Stavanger in the south and Kristiansund in the north.

Two of the fjords in this part of the country have been included on UNESCO's World Culture and Natural Heritage List.

These are the 17-kilometre long Nærøyfjord and the 15-kilometre long Geirangerfjord.

They are known as the narrowest, wildest and most spectacular fjords in the world and are good representatives for the dramatic fjord landscape, which otherwise characterises this part of the country.

Also in Western Norway's fjord landscape lie 20 of the country's largest glaciers, in addition to many of Norway's highest mountains. Jostedalsbreen is the largest glacier on the European mainland with its 480 km².

In many other places in Western Norway you can find traces of old settlements, for example, from Viking times. The Norwegian stave churches are architectual monuments that commemorate the introduction of Christianity in Norway. Borgrund Stave Church and Urnes Stave Church are both situated on the branches of Sognefjord and can be dated back to the 12th and 13th centuries.

A network of ferry connections, bridges, tunnels and steeply ascending roads up the faces of mountains link the fjord kingdom of Western Norway together. Whether you travel by water or land, you will have a dramatic experience where nature is the sole entertainer. An excursion on the narrow and winding roads up the steep mountains or a boat trip on the fjord will take your breath away and give you a lifelong experience.

084 Early in the morning by the Pulpit Rock (Preikestolen), which towers over Lysefjord. This is the southernmost fjord in Western Norway.
085 Fruit blossom in Hardanger, Norway's fruit garden.
086 During summer, many of the fjords and lakes turn green from melting water from the glaciers, such as is seen here at Oldevatnet.
087 Cyclists on Kjeragbolten, which is a stone wedged in a ravine by Lysefjord.
088 Folgefonna is Norway's third largest glacier and a wonderful place for glacier hiking.

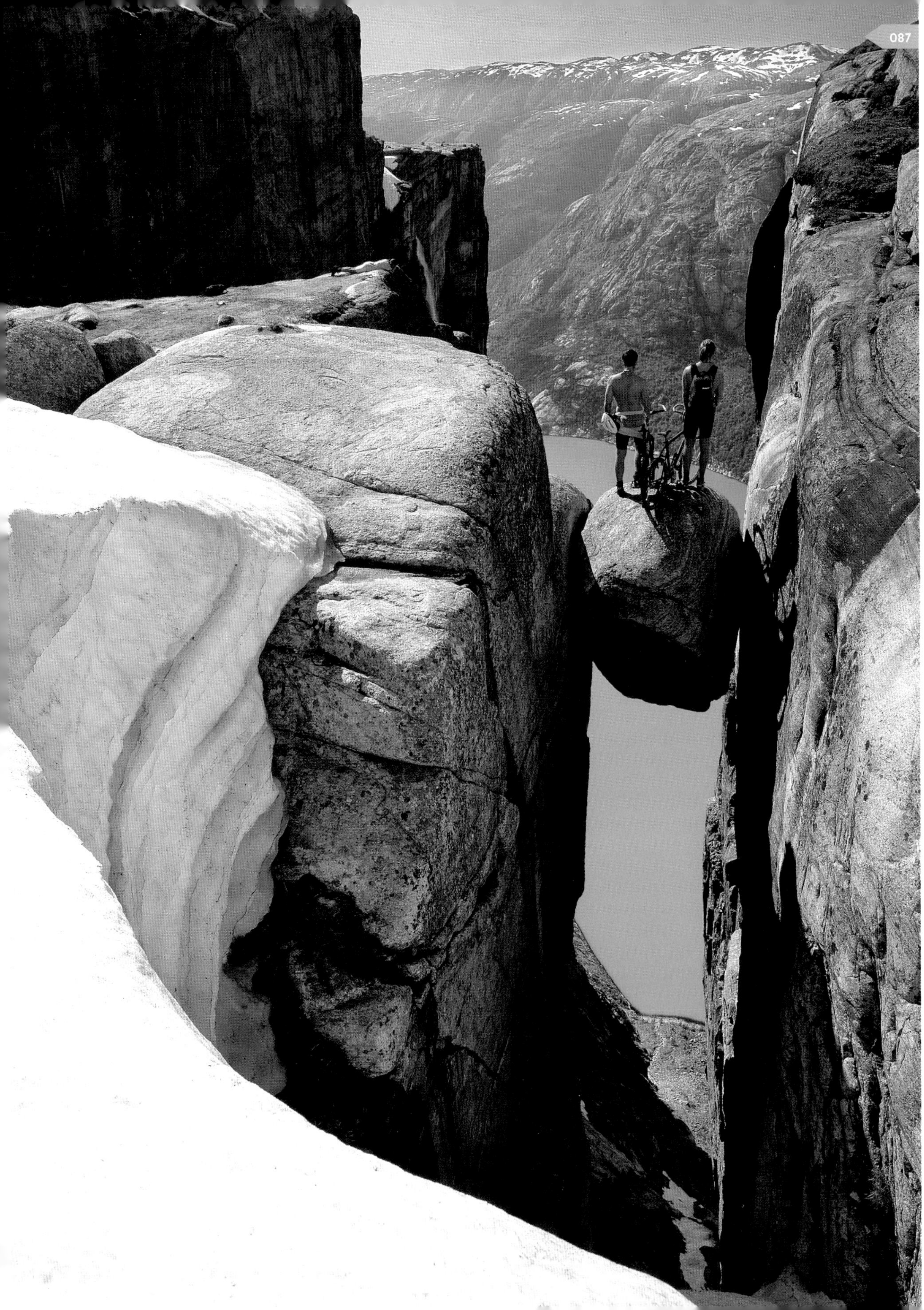

089 The picturesque mountain farm, Kjeåsen in Eidfjord,
Hardanger.
090 Ferry traffic at Utne in Hardanger.
091 If it is the right season, you can see the beautiful rose garden at
Baroniet in Rosendal in Hardanger.
092 The impressive Vøringsfossen Waterfall in Eidfjord,
Hardanger, is one of Norway's most visited nature attractions.
The waterfall cascades 182 metres in total.

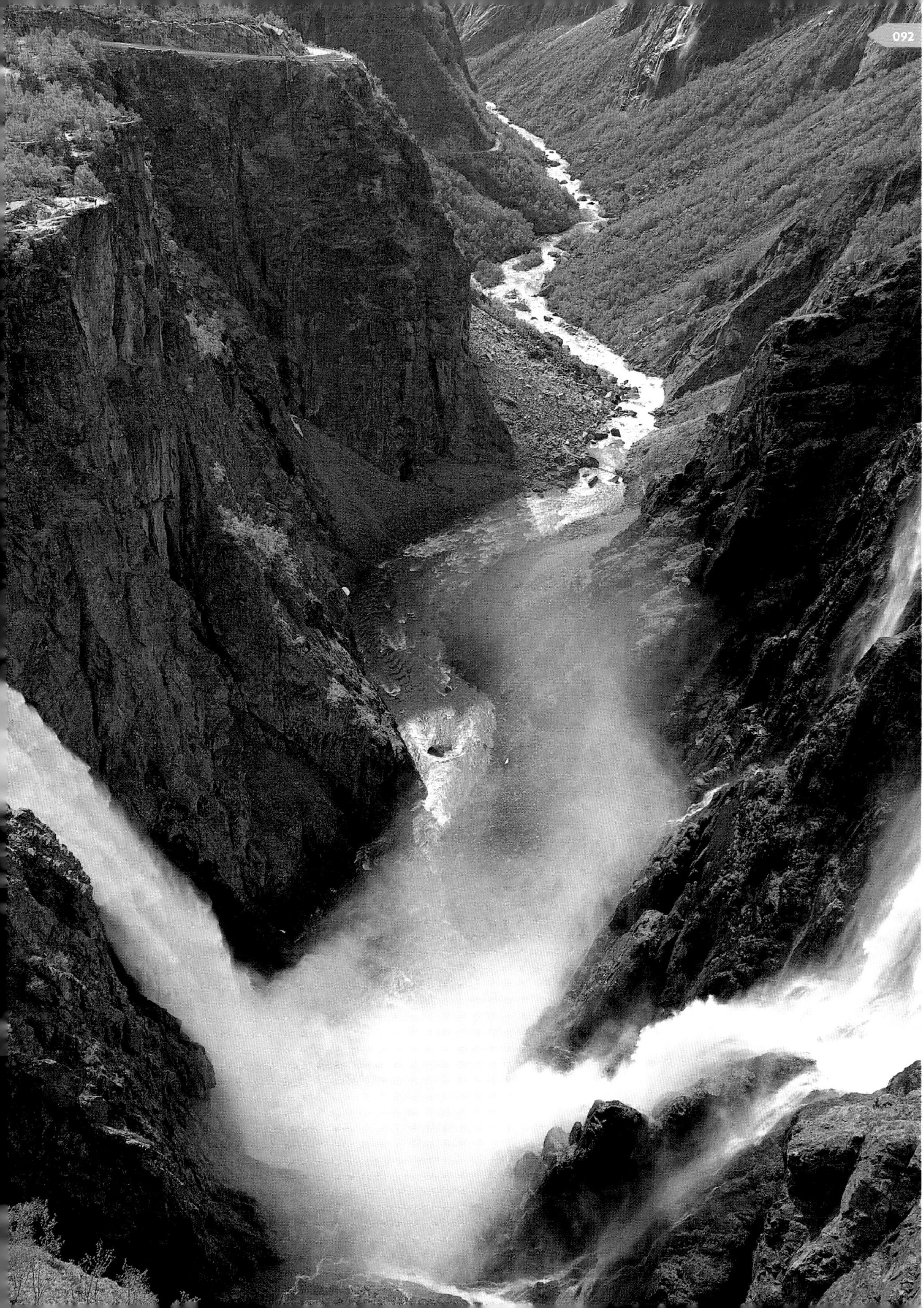

093 View point from Stegastein over Sognefjord.
094 Flåm is a busy cruise ship port during the summer season.
095 Låtefoss Waterfall in Odda is one of Norway's most visited
nature-based tourist attractions.
096 The Aurlandsfjord.
097 The Flåm Railway is one of the world's most spectacular
railway lines. It takes 55 minutes for the train to travel
the two miles from Myrdal on the Bergen Railway into
Hardangervidda. First the train will take you up to the 900
metre tree line and then down to Flåm by the Aurlandsfjord.
098 The 17 km long and narrow Nærøyfjord is a branch of the
Sognefjord and is included on UNESCO'S World Heritage List.

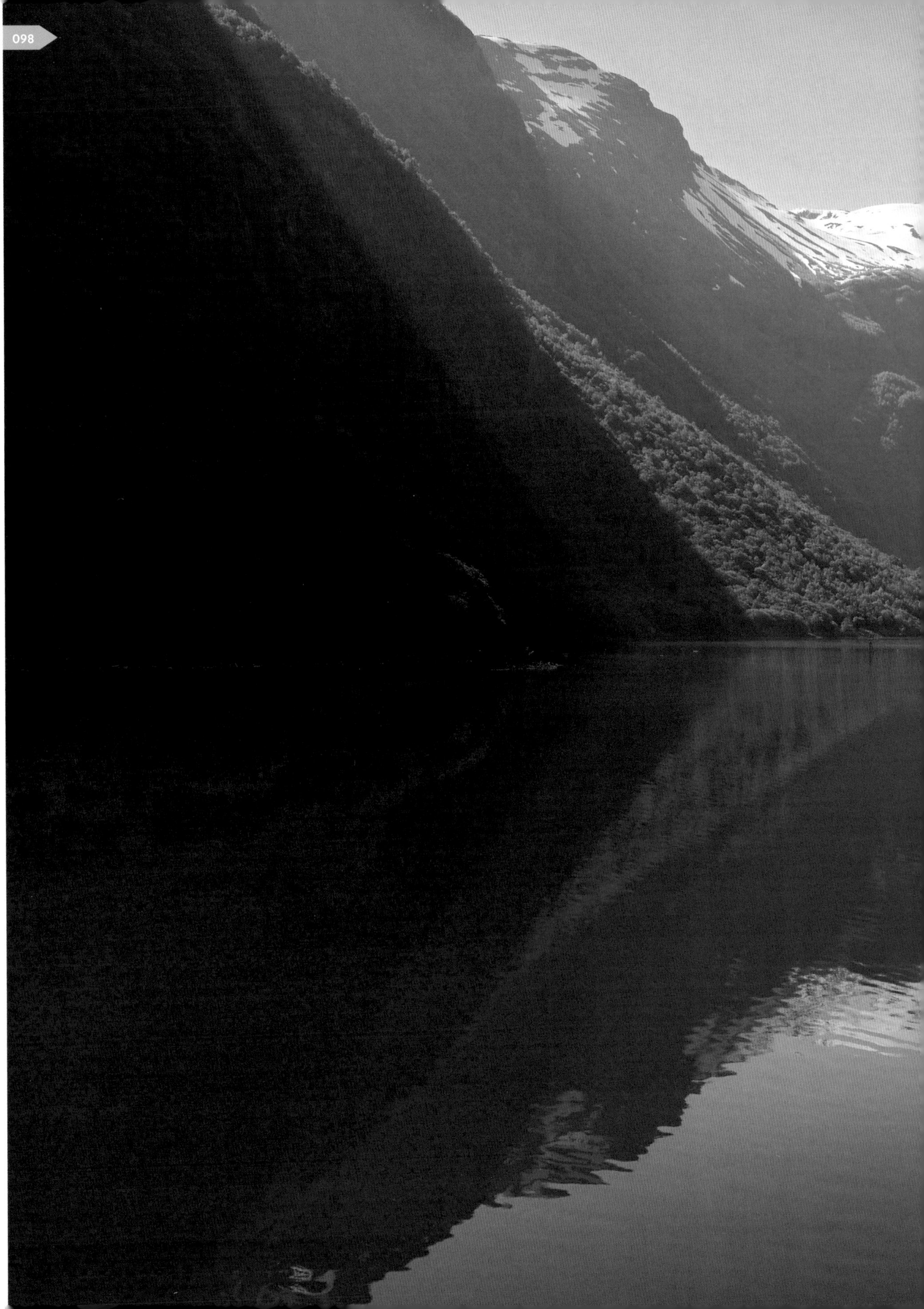

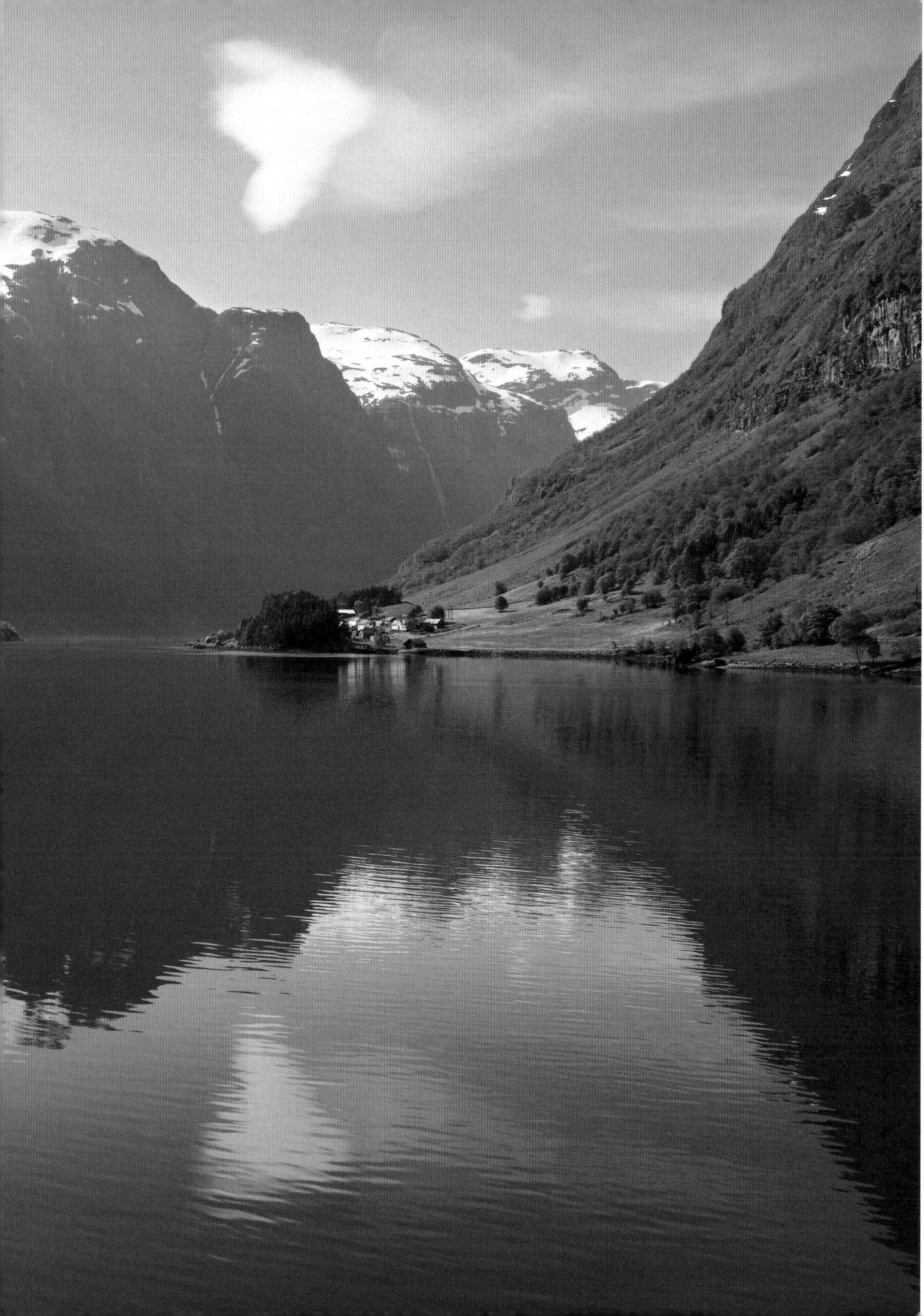

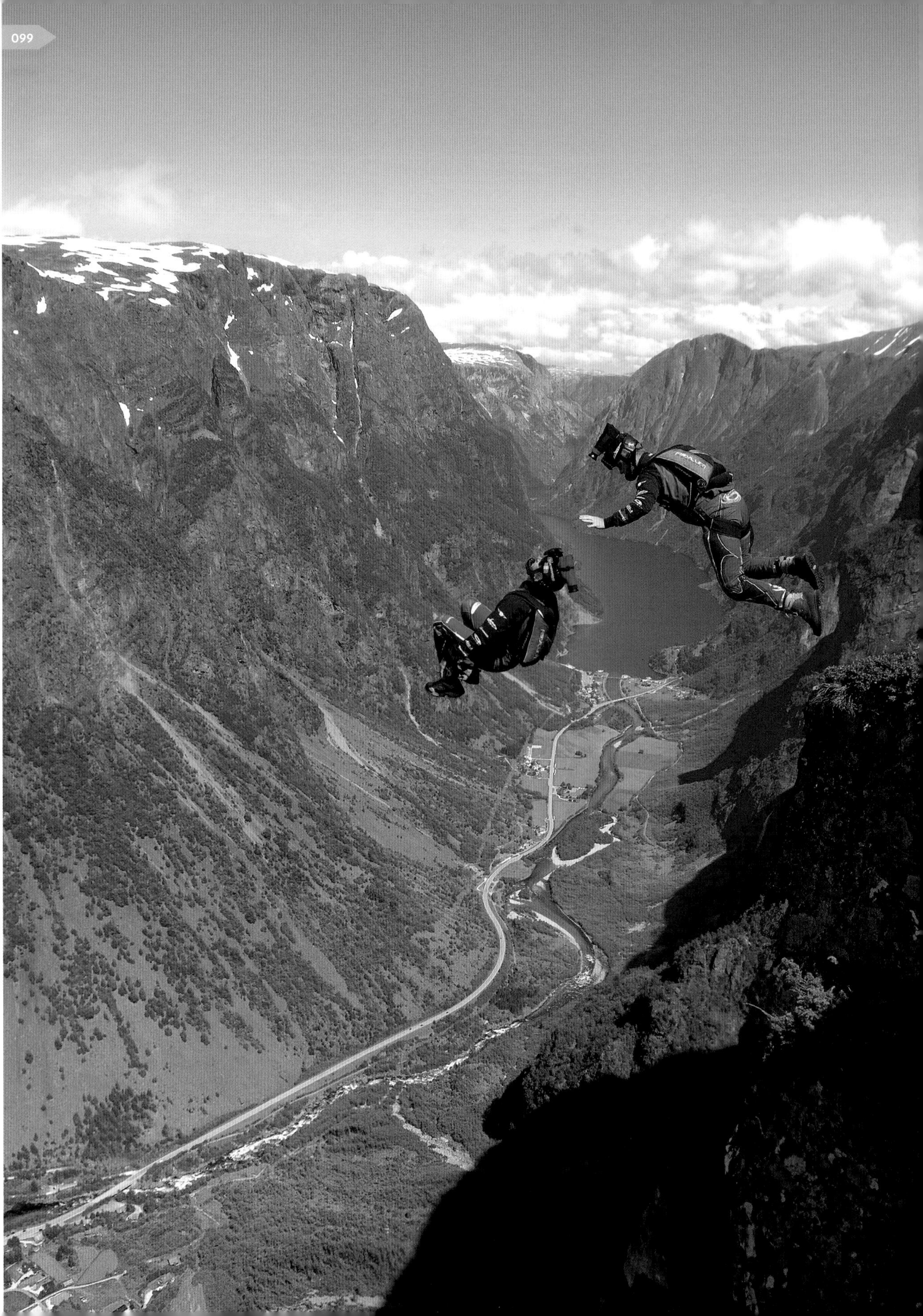

099 Base jumpers in acrobatic leaps from Nebbet in Gudvangen.

100 Urnes stave church by Lustrafjord is one of Norway's oldest preserved stave churches from the first half of the 1100s. The church has been included on UNESCO's World Cultural Heritage List.

101 Borgund stave church lies in Lærdal, innermost in Sognefjord, and is estimated to be the best preserved of the Norwegian stave churches from the Middle Ages. Most of the Norwegian stave churches were erected between 1150 and 1350. Only 28 stand today.

102 Urnes stave church is richly decorated inside. Here you can see the ornaments from the churches external walls.

103   Briksdal Glacier is a branch of the Jostedal Glacier.
104   Cattle by Breng Summer Mountain Farm by Lovatnet.
105   Tourists on a glacier excursion on Briksdal Glacier.
106   Sheep on Grotli over the Strynefjellet Mountains.
107   View of Ålesund. Following the great city fire in 1904, the city
      was rebuilt, and over a few years approximately 350 buildings
      were erected in the characteristic Jugend style. Today the city
      has one of the most stunning and visually complete city cores
      in Norway.

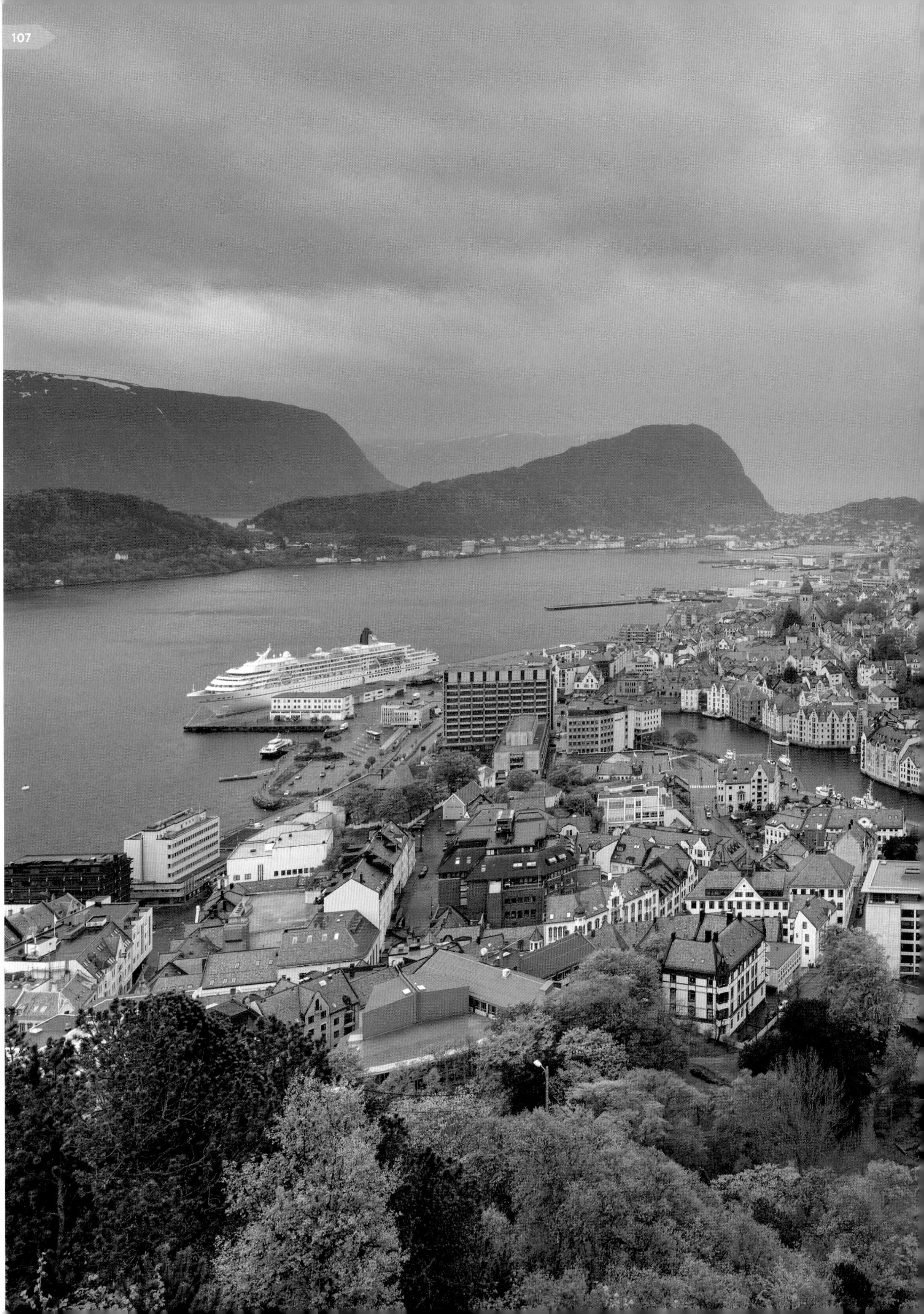

108 Brosundet in the Centre of Ålesund.
109 Ålesund's characteristic buildings in Jugend style.
110 Atlantic Puffins on the bird mountain on the Isle of Runde.
111 View towards Geirangerfjord from Flydalsjuvet.

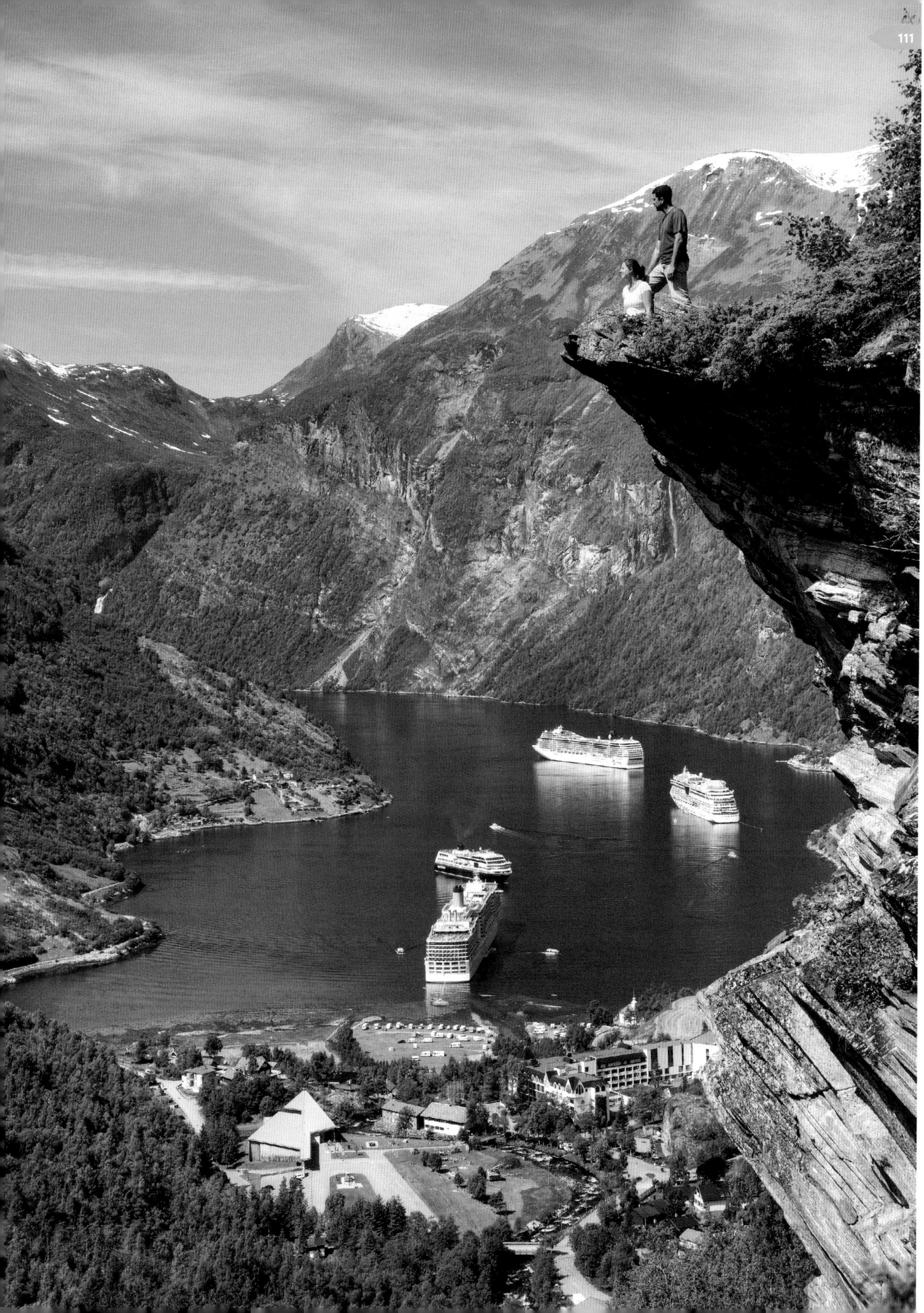

111

112 With trendsetting architecture, Gudbrandsjuvet was given a new look in 2010 in connection with the National Tourist Routes project.

113 Trollstigen is the most known tourist route in Norway. In parts the road is narrow and steep, and it has 11 hairpin bends.

114 From Mount Dalsnibba (1476 metres above seal level) you have a good view down to Geirangerfjord.

115 Along Geirangerfjord are waterfalls, such as the Suitor (Friaren), the Seven Sisters (De syv søstre) and the Wedding Veil (Brudesløret).

116 The Hurtigruten ship in Geirangerfjord, a must on the 'world's most beautiful sea voyage' going northwards to Kirkenes.

117 In a mountain slope high above Geirangerfjord lies the abandoned Skagaflå Mountain Farm with a view of the Seven Sisters (De syv søstre) waterfalls.

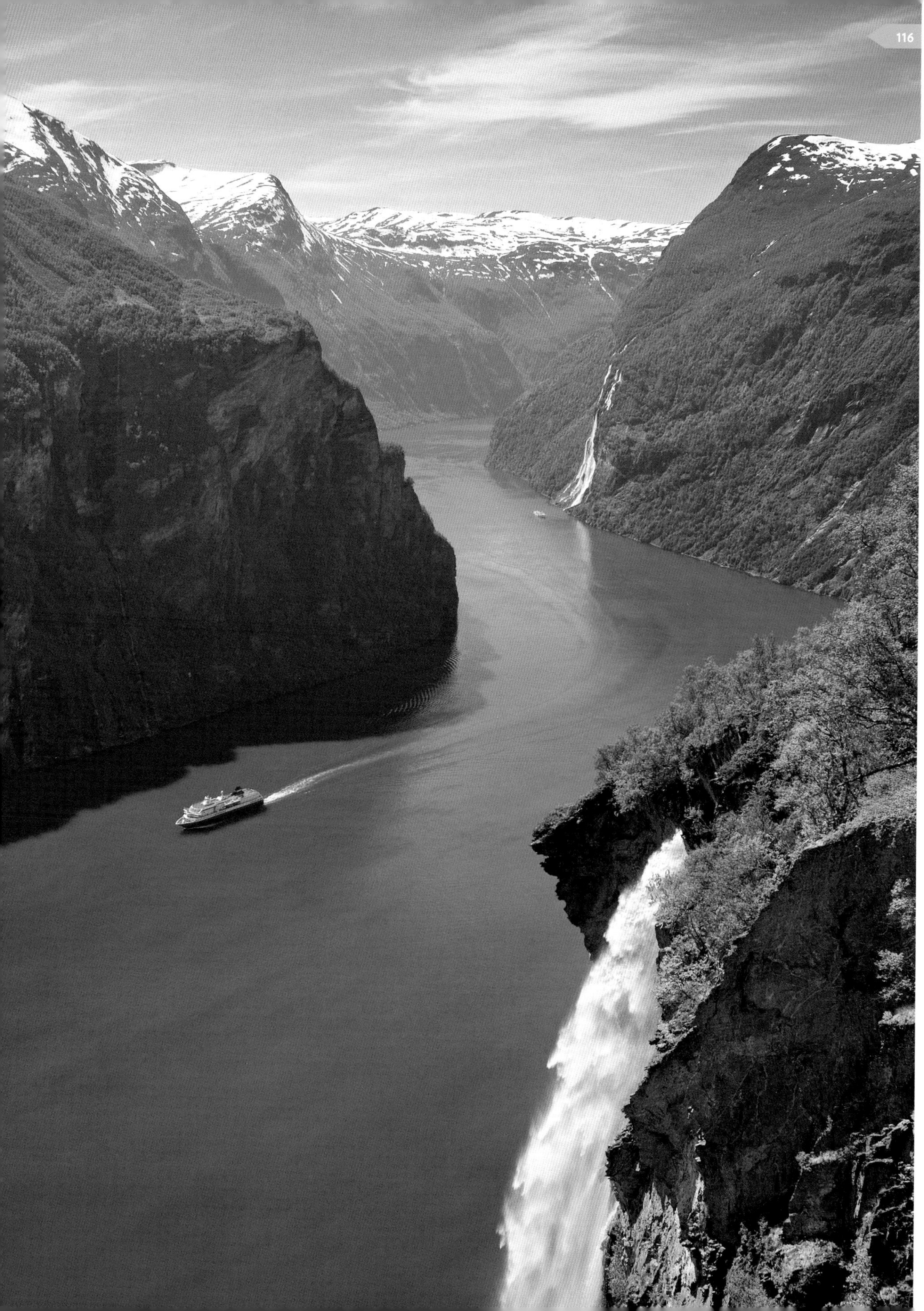

116

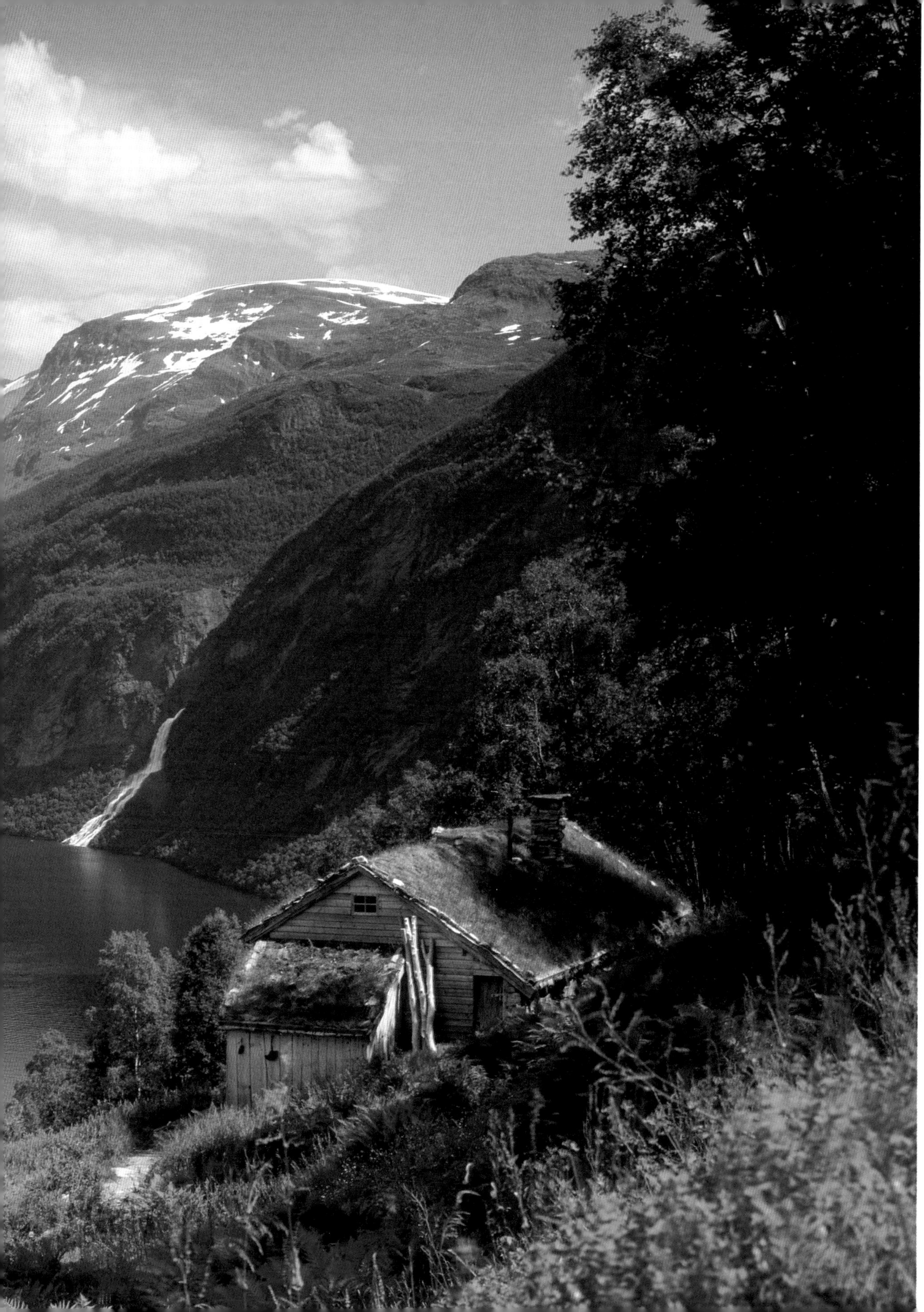

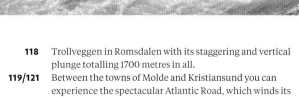

118 Trollveggen in Romsdalen with its staggering and vertical plunge totalling 1700 metres in all.

119/121 Between the towns of Molde and Kristiansund you can experience the spectacular Atlantic Road, which winds its way from island to island with the mighty sea as its nearest neighbour.

120 Tourist bus going over the Stigfossen Waterfall in Trollstigen.

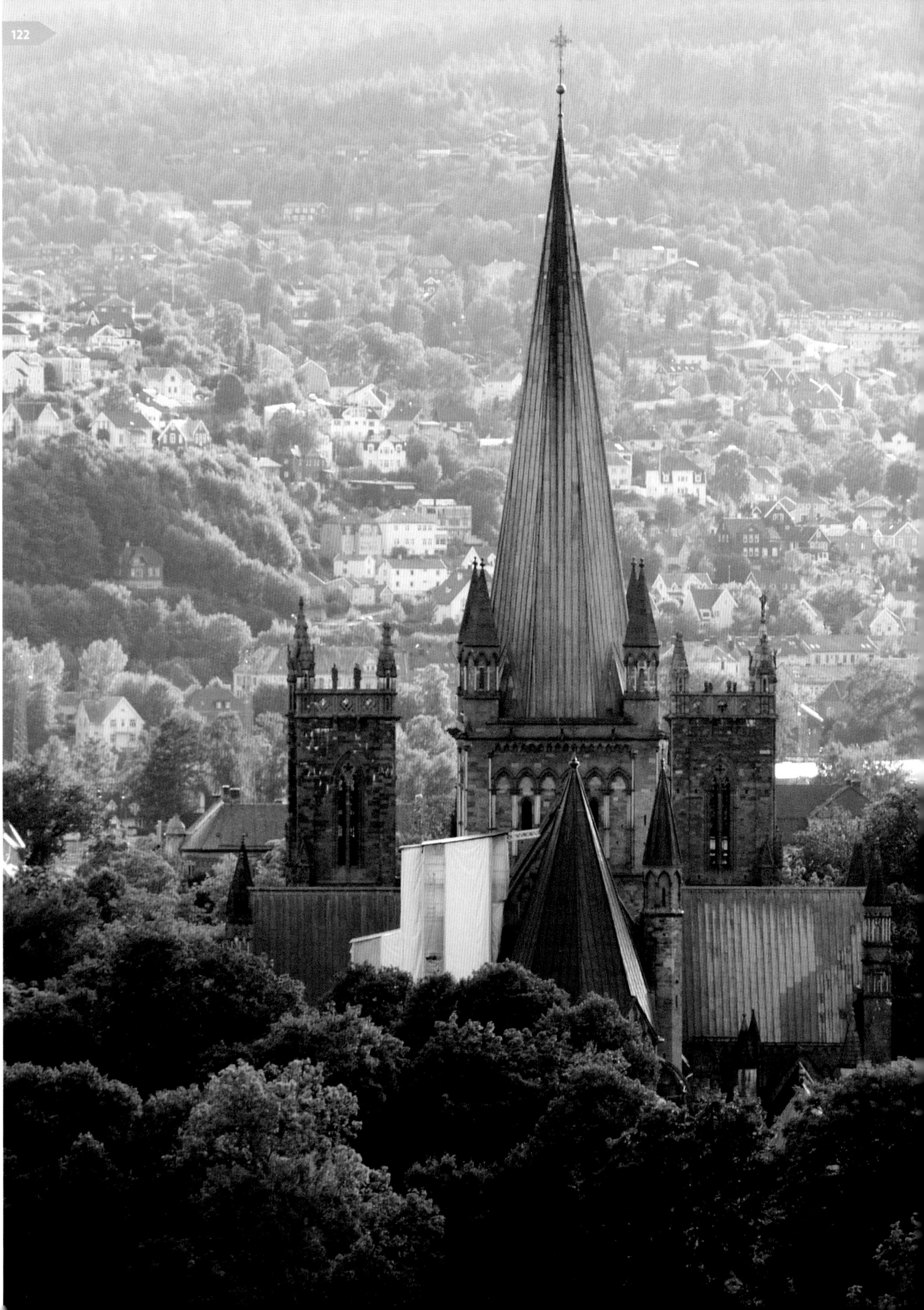
122

TRONDHEIM – THE PILGRIM'S DESTINATION

Nidaros Cathedral is the landmark of Trondheim and the largest cathedral in the Nordic countries. Pilgrims have gone on pilgrimages here in their search of Olav the Holy's grave for almost a thousand years. Today's travellers also hike or cycle on the old pilgrim routes. Others go on pilgrimages to other and more worldly shrines – the large fishing rivers, which lie in the areas around the city.

Trondheim, the former Norwegian capital, is now the third largest city with over 181,000 inhabitants.

Trondheim, or Nidaros as the city was previously called, was founded by Olav Tryggvason in 997 AD.

In 1030 AD Olav the Holy was killed in the Battle of Stiklestad. As a result Christianity became firmly established in Norway.

Initially a small wooden chapel was built over Olav's grave; afterwards the people built a stone church, which was the first stage of the cathedral we know today.

A large number of gifts were given to the church as Olav the Holy's reputation as a saint rapidly spread. He became the country's greatest martyr-king and was known and worshipped far beyond the borders of Norway.

In the Middle Ages, Nidaros was actually the most popular pilgramage site in Northern Europe. Today the country's crown jewels are stored in Nidaros Cathedral along with church treasures from earlier ages.

Trondheim offers many other sights and experiences, among these the charming timber development at Bakklandet and the special wharves at the mouth of the river Nidelven. Many cultural monuments tell the story of the city's historical importance, however even with all its historical roots, Trondheim is still a modern city. Not to mention that the city by the river Nidelven is also a university city and the capital of technology in Norway.

Some of the country's most lush agricultural villages are found along Trondheimfjord. And nowhere else are so many petroglyphs found as in the areas around Trondheim.

You can feel the atmosphere from the dramatic past in the Trondheim cultural landscape in a positive way.

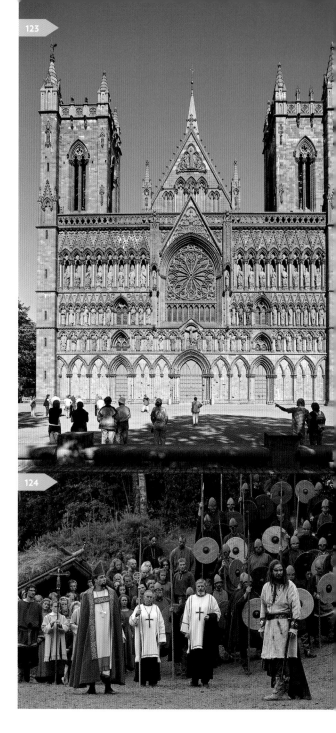

122 Nidaros Cathedral dominates Trondheim's urban horizon.
123 Trondheim and the west wall of Nidaros Cathedral, which is the cathedral's most beautiful and richest side.
124 The Stiklestad play tells the story of Olav the Holy and the Christianisation of Norway. The outdoor performance is staged every year close to Verdal, north of Trondheim.
125 Details on Nidaros Cathedral.
126 The statue portrays Olav Tryggvason, who was one of the most central and influential Norwegian kings. It stands in the square in the Centre of Trondheim.
127 Early morning by the wharves on the Nidelven River in Trondheim.

NORTHERN NORWAY – THE KINGDOM OF THE MIDNIGHT SUN

Northern Norway's wild nature is spellbinding with the sight of mountains, the sea, mountain plateaus and fjords. The midnight sun and northern lights are so magnificent that it can take the most travelled person's breath away. And between the high mountains and numerous islands lies the charming fishing villages with their fishermen shacks.

This northern part of Norway equates to a third of Norway, but only 10 percent of the Norwegian population live here. Most of the people here live in one of the many quaint small towns along the coast. The larger areas with untouched nature span from mountain plateaus with grazing tame reindeer and a multitude of fishing waters to steep mountain peaks, fjords and numerous areas with skerries along the coast.

Areas to the north of the Arctic Circle are dark in the middle of winter and in the summer they are lit up with the midnight sun.

The best way to arrive in Northern Norway is by boat. Hurtigruten or Riksvei 1 (national road) as it is also called, starts from Bergen in the south and goes all the way to Kirkenes in the north. On the way to the north you will cross the Arctic Circle before you reach the Lofoten mountains, which rise from the sea like a majestic wall.

Folklore says that these are the oldest mountains in the world. Lofoten is an archipelago and perhaps the most popular tourist attraction in this part of Norway. It has always been one of the most fish rich areas in the world.

Hurtigruten calls at all the towns and cities along the northern Norway coastline, among others the 'capital' of this part of the country, Tromsø, which lies to the north of Lofoten. Quite rightly, the city became known as the Paris of the North due to its various restaurants, bars, night clubs and cafes. The wonderful Arctic Cathedral also lies here.

The nature in Northern Norway is among the most untouched in Europe. The conditions are more extreme here than further south in Norway, and it has been necessary for people to adapt to the landscape and forces of nature. You can experience the forces of nature at close hand by living in a Sami tipi on the Finnmark plateau or in a fisherman's shack in Lofoten.

Wild nature attracts mountain climbers, glacier hikers and skiers.

Along the coastal route on the way to Bodø on Hurtigruten you can see the Svartisen Glacier, which creeps down to the sea, or experience killer whales as they play around the boat.

Or how about an excursion to the Finnmark Plateau, (the home of the Sami people) by reindeer, if desired?

The plateau also boasts 60,000 fishing lakes and thousands of kilometres of salmon and trout rivers.

From the North Cape, Europe's northernmost point, you can look over the Barents Sea in the direction of Svalbard and the North Pole.

128 Early morning in Reine in Lofoten.

129 Nordland style house by Mount Torghatten near Brønnøysund in Nordland.

130 Northern Norway has a rich bird life, represented here by a seagull *(Larus canus)*.

131 Hurtigrute Ship Nordlys with Mount Torghatten in Nordland in the background. Mount Torghatten has a hole through its centre. The hole is 160 metres long, 35 metres high and 20 metres wide.

132 The northern lights are a natural phenomen which occurs in polar regions and can be seen in the sky as a wavy light. The northern lights vary in shape, strength and colour from navy blue to green and yellow, and red and orange.

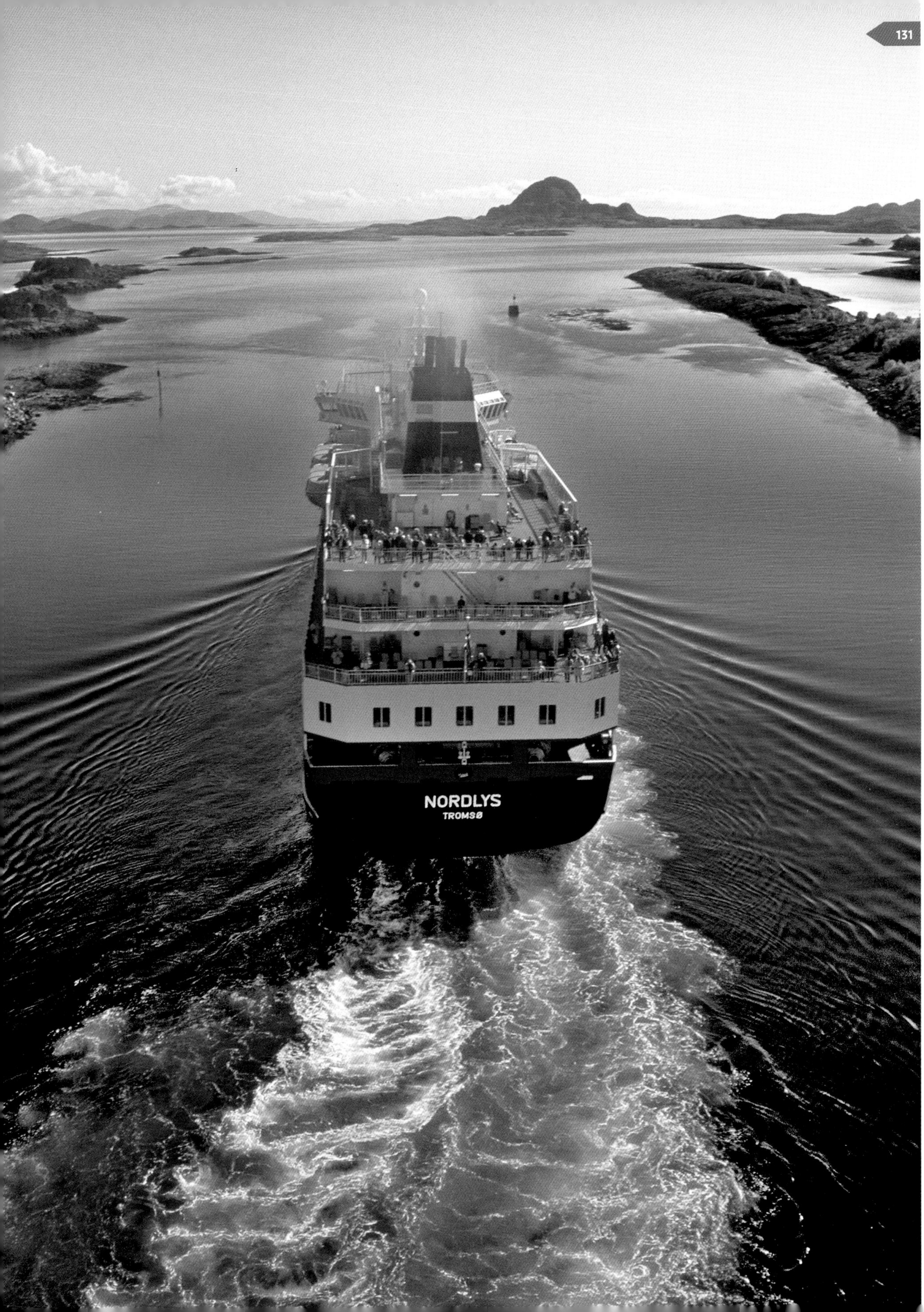
NORDLYS
TROMSØ

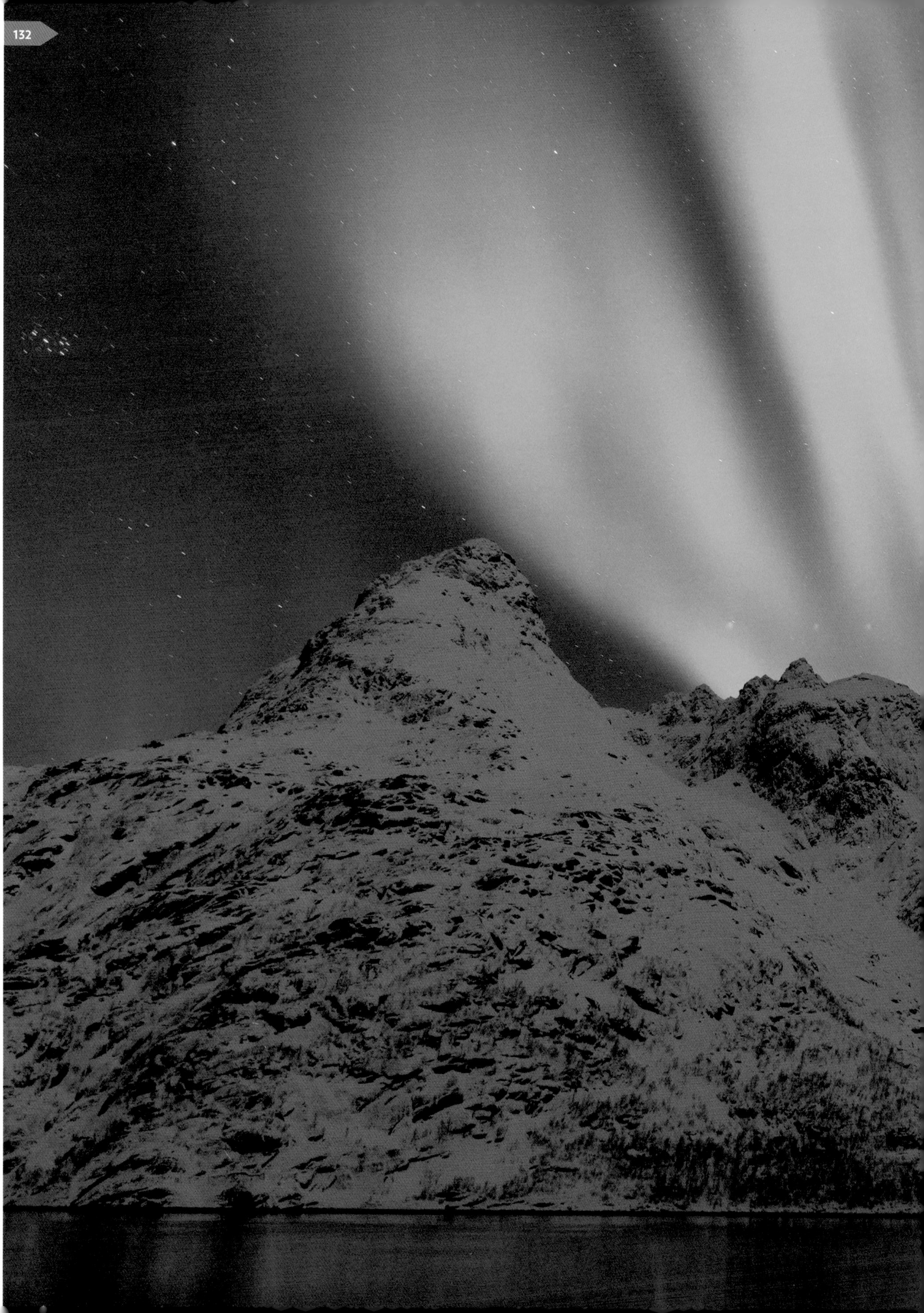

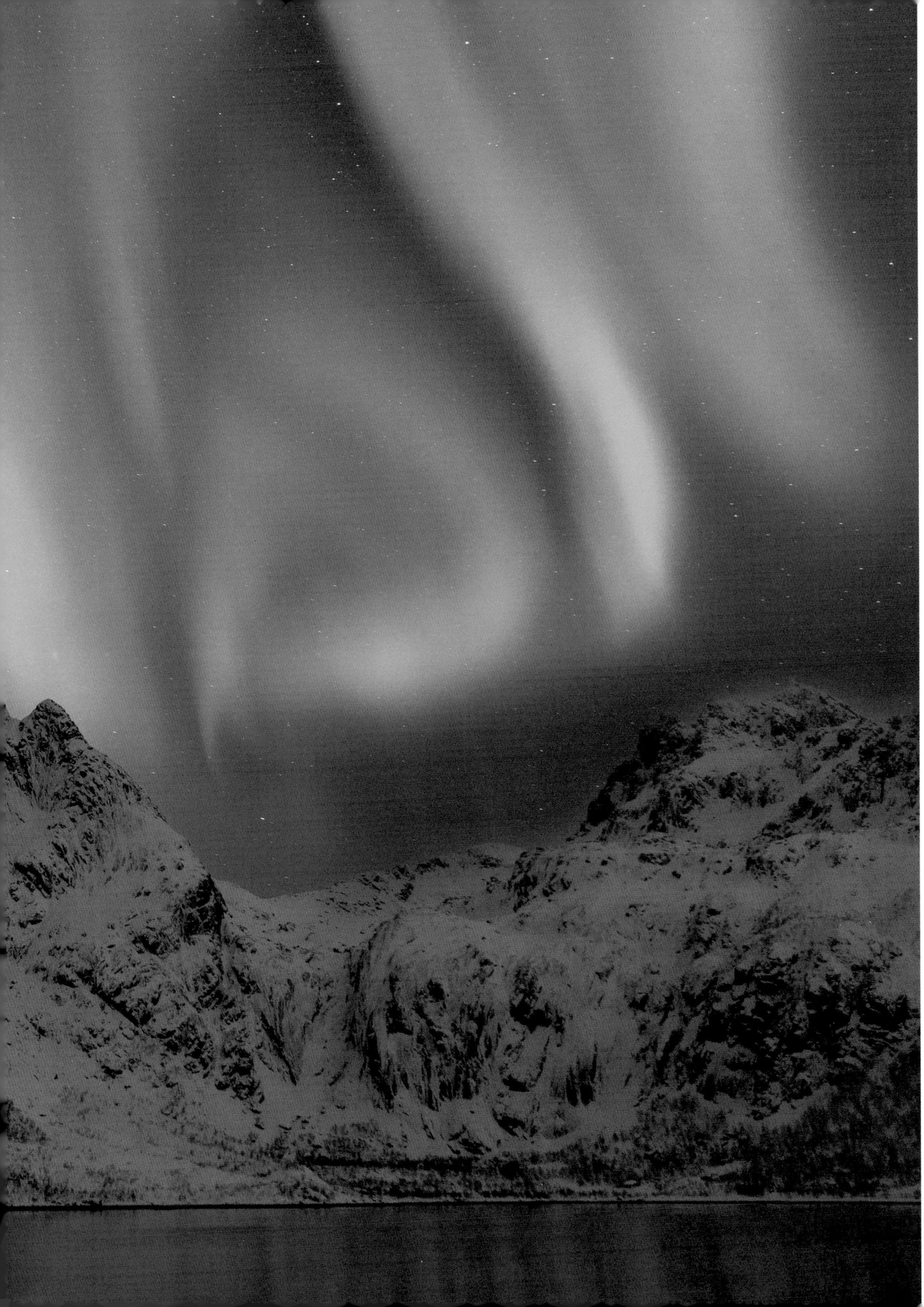

134

135

133 A common eider's bird house on one of the Vega islands in Nordland. The 6500 islands, islets and skerries in the area have been included on UNESCO's World Cultural and Natural Heritage List due to the archipelago's unique coastal culture. Since the Stone Age people have lived with extreme weather conditions south of the Arctic Circle when fishing and collecting eggs, and gathering the very soft eider feathers.

134 The Arctic Circle Centre at Saltfjellet Mountain in Bodø in Nordland. Adjacent to this is the Saltfjellet-Svartisen National Park. The Arctic Circle is the gateway to Arctic Norway where you can experience the midnight sun and full season of darkness.

135 Eider *(Somateria mollissima)* in flight.
136 Cyclists on Herøy on the Helgeland Coast. The Seven Sisters' mountain range in the background.
137 Atlantic Puffins under the midnight sun. The Isle of Træna in the background is Norway's oldest fishing village.

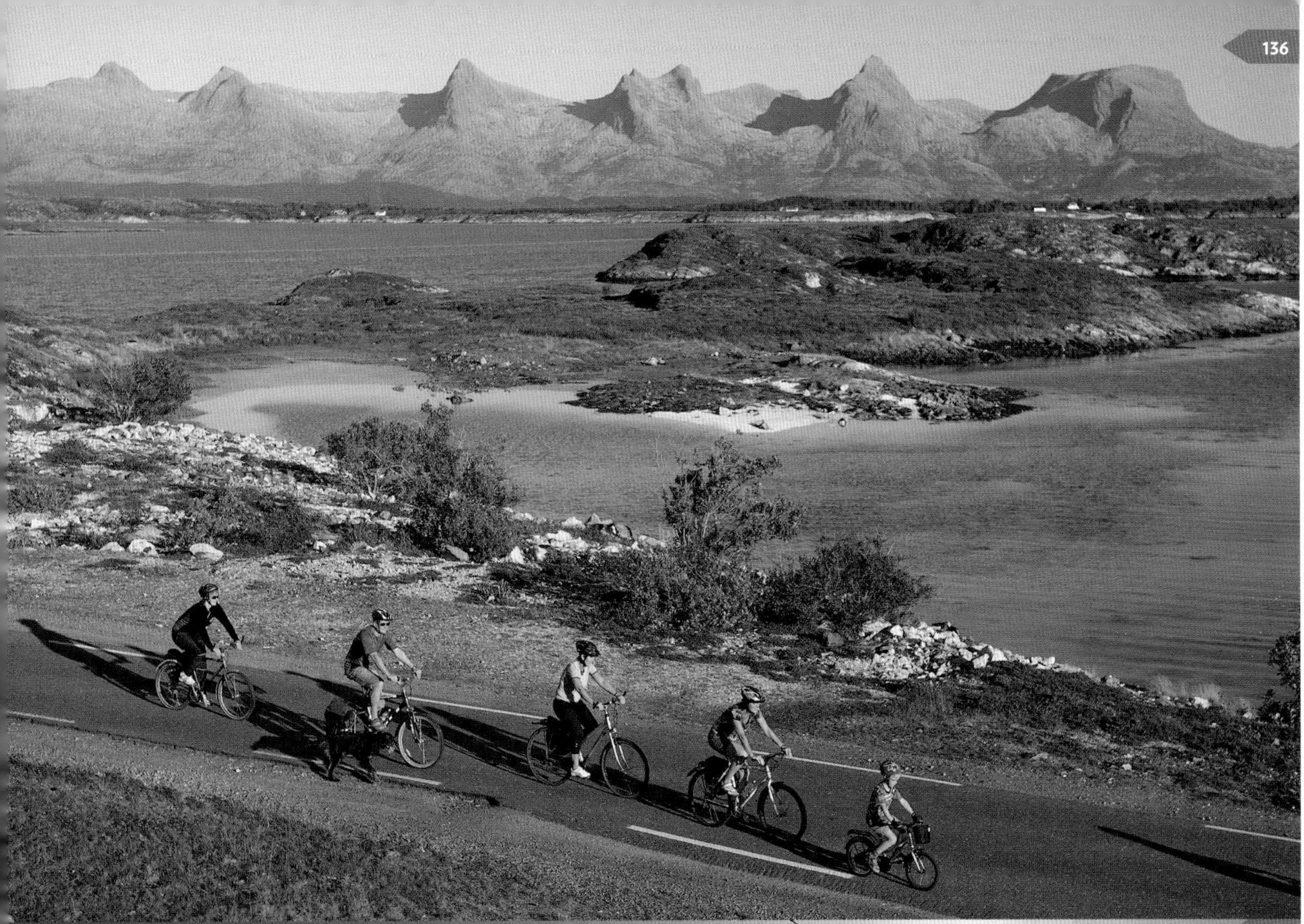

136

137

141

142

138 Svartisen Glacier.

139 Tourists by Austerdalsisen Glacier, a branch of the Svartisen Glacier.

140 The old trading building on beautiful Kjerringøy, north of Bodø.

141 Saltstraumen is the world's strongest tidal current and one of the most stunning diving destinations in the world.

142 Saltstraumen is one of the best places in Norway to fish, thanks to oxygen rich water.

144

146

143 The Hamsun Centre on Hamarøy where writer Knut Hamsun grew up. He is seen as one of the most influential writers from the 1900s and many consider him to be the inventor of the modern novel. The Hamsun Centre was opened on Hamsun's 150th birthday in 2009.

144 A summer's day on Moskenesøy Island in Lofoten.

145 View from Reinebrinken in Lofoten.

146 Reine fishing village in Lofoten.

147 A cruise ship entering the narrow Trollfjord, which is only
about 70 metres wide at its mouth.
148 Atlantic Puffin on the Isle of Røst at the furthermost point in
Lofoten.
149 Mountain climbers on Mount Svolværgeita, Svolvær in
Lofoten.
150 A summer's day in innermost Vestvågøy in Lofoten.

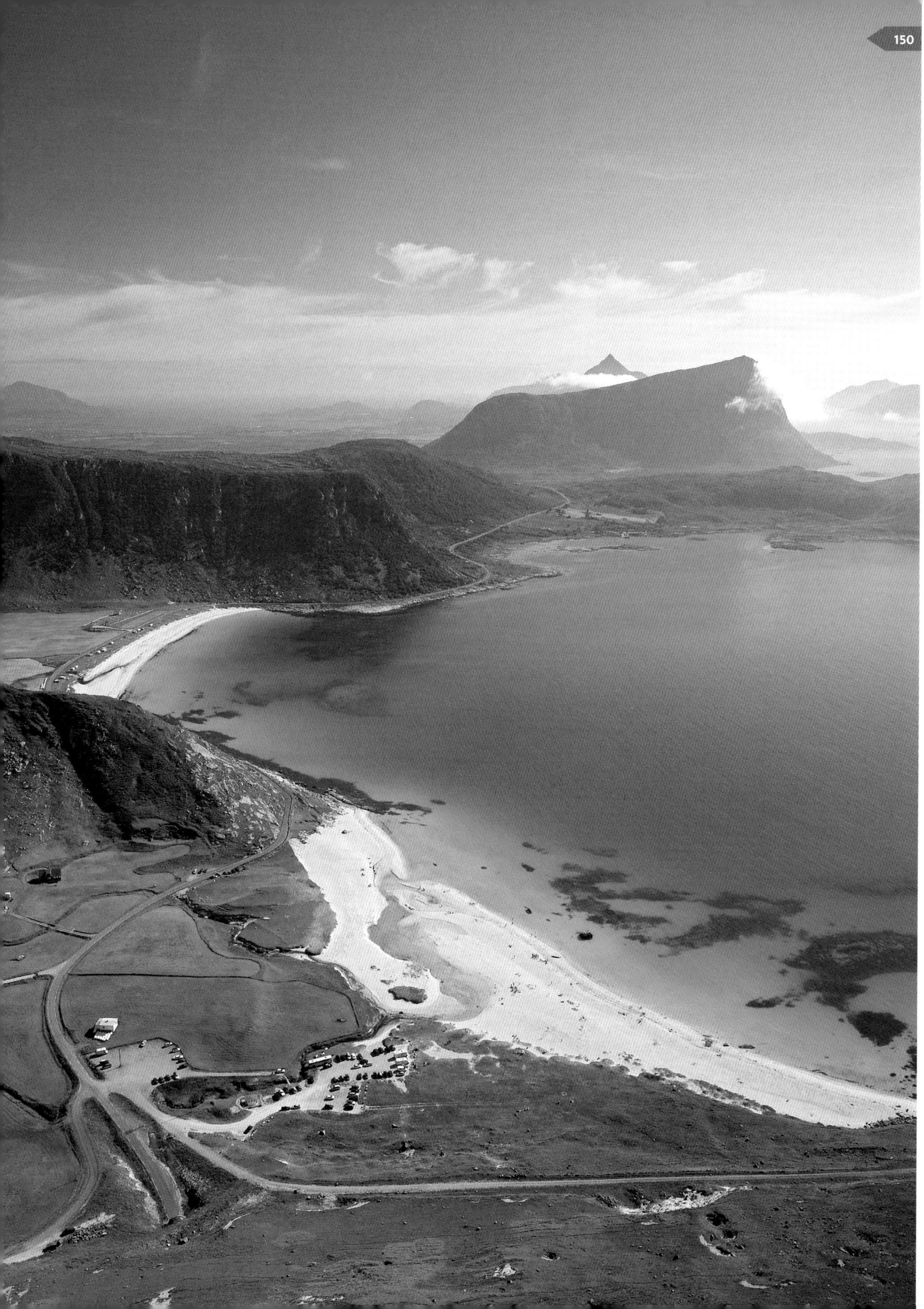

150

151

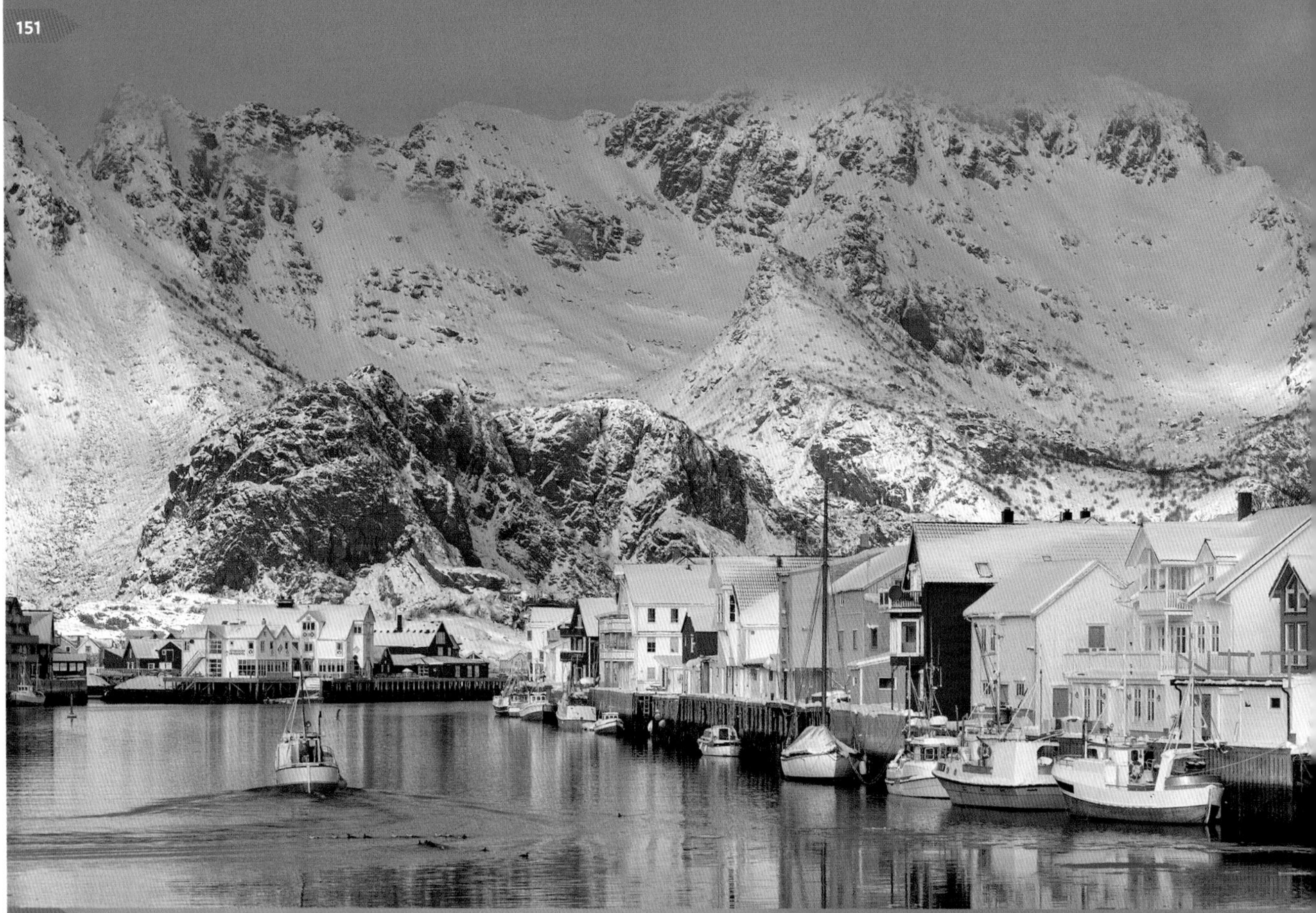

152

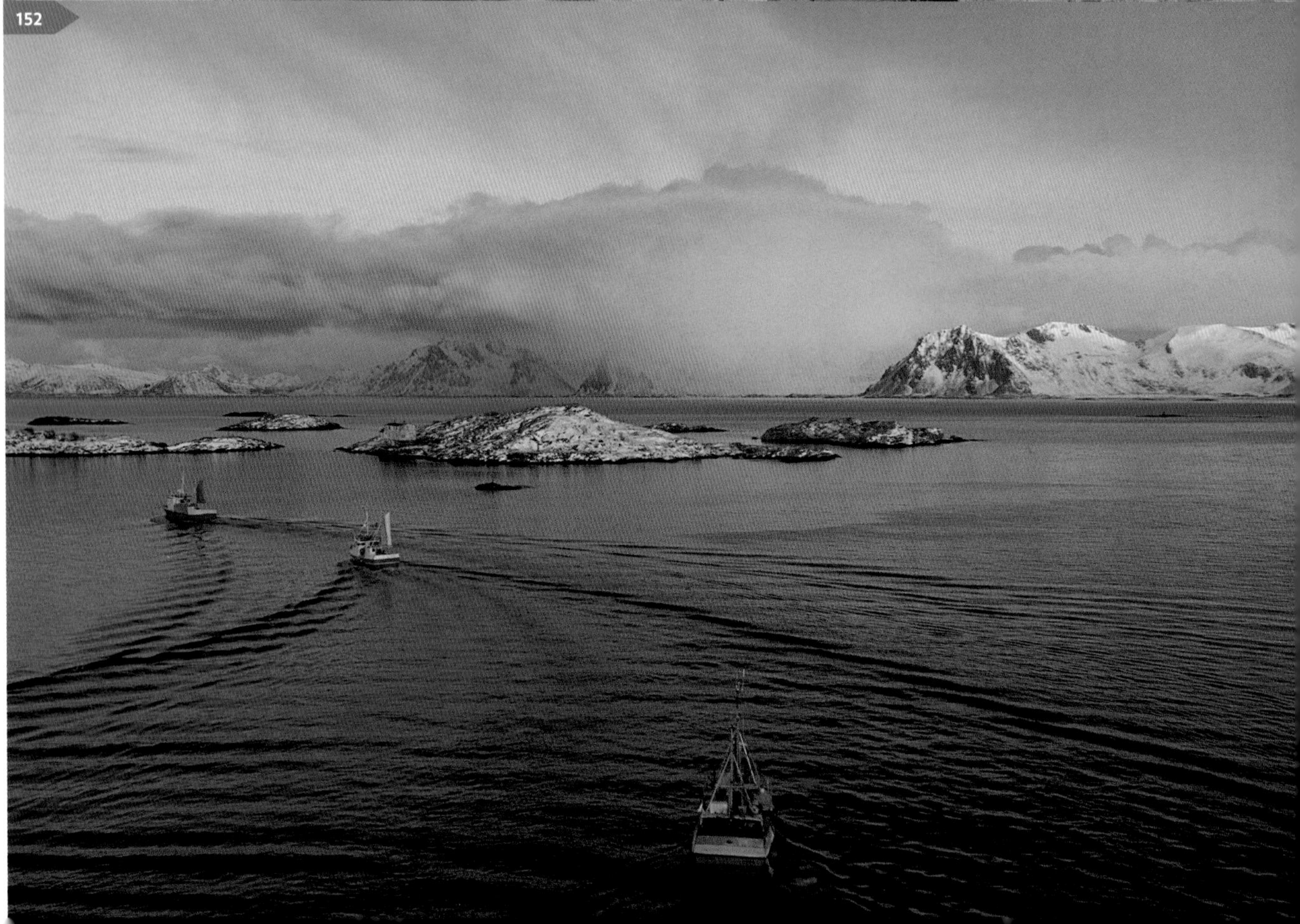

151   A winter's day in Henningsvær in Lofoten.

152   The tough Lofoten fishing season has been crucial to the local community, as well as the entire nation. Cod fishing is done during the winter when the fish approach the coastline to spawn.

153   A fisherman pulls a large cod to land.

154   The cod is hung to dry on fish racks in Lofoten.

155

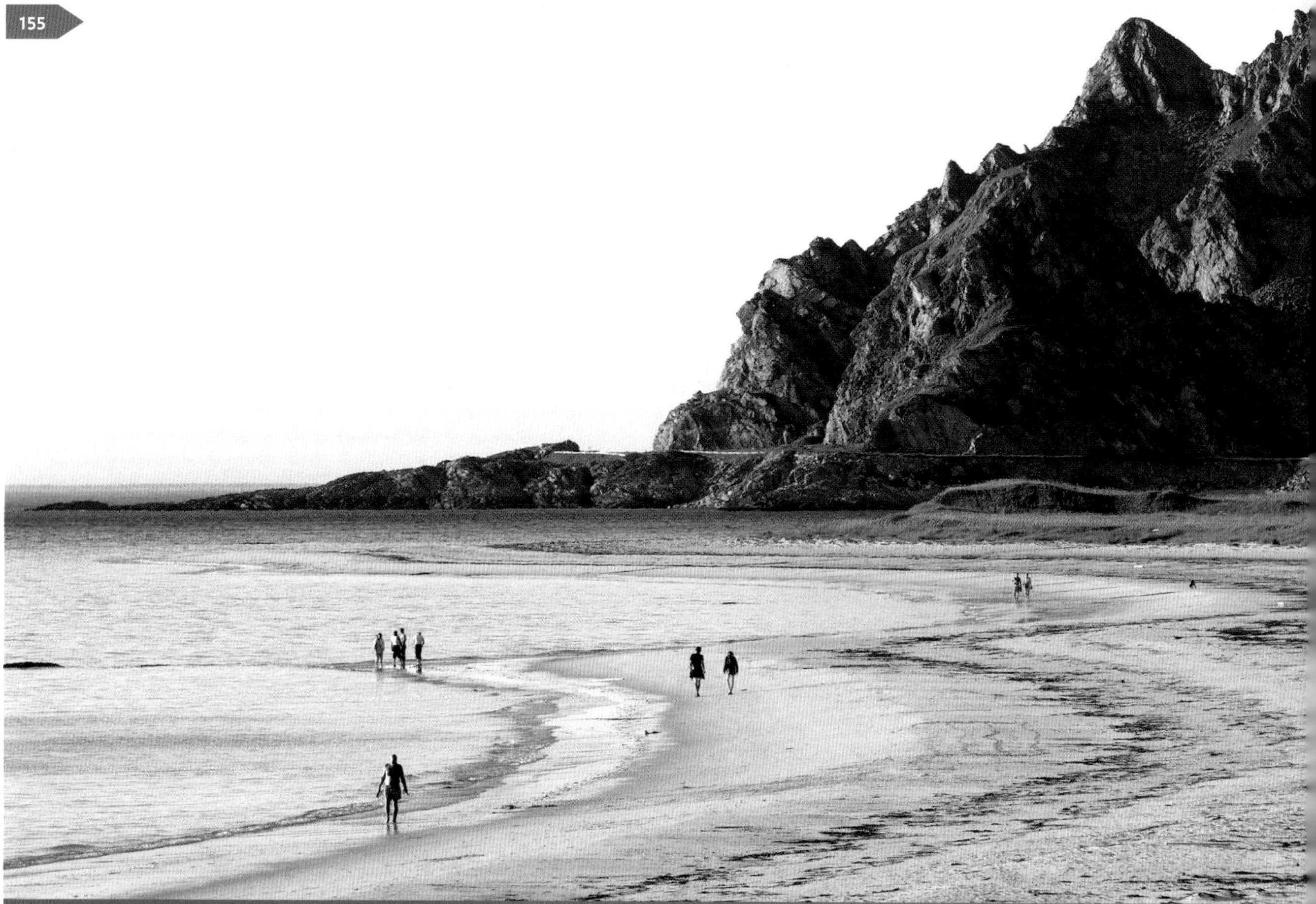

156

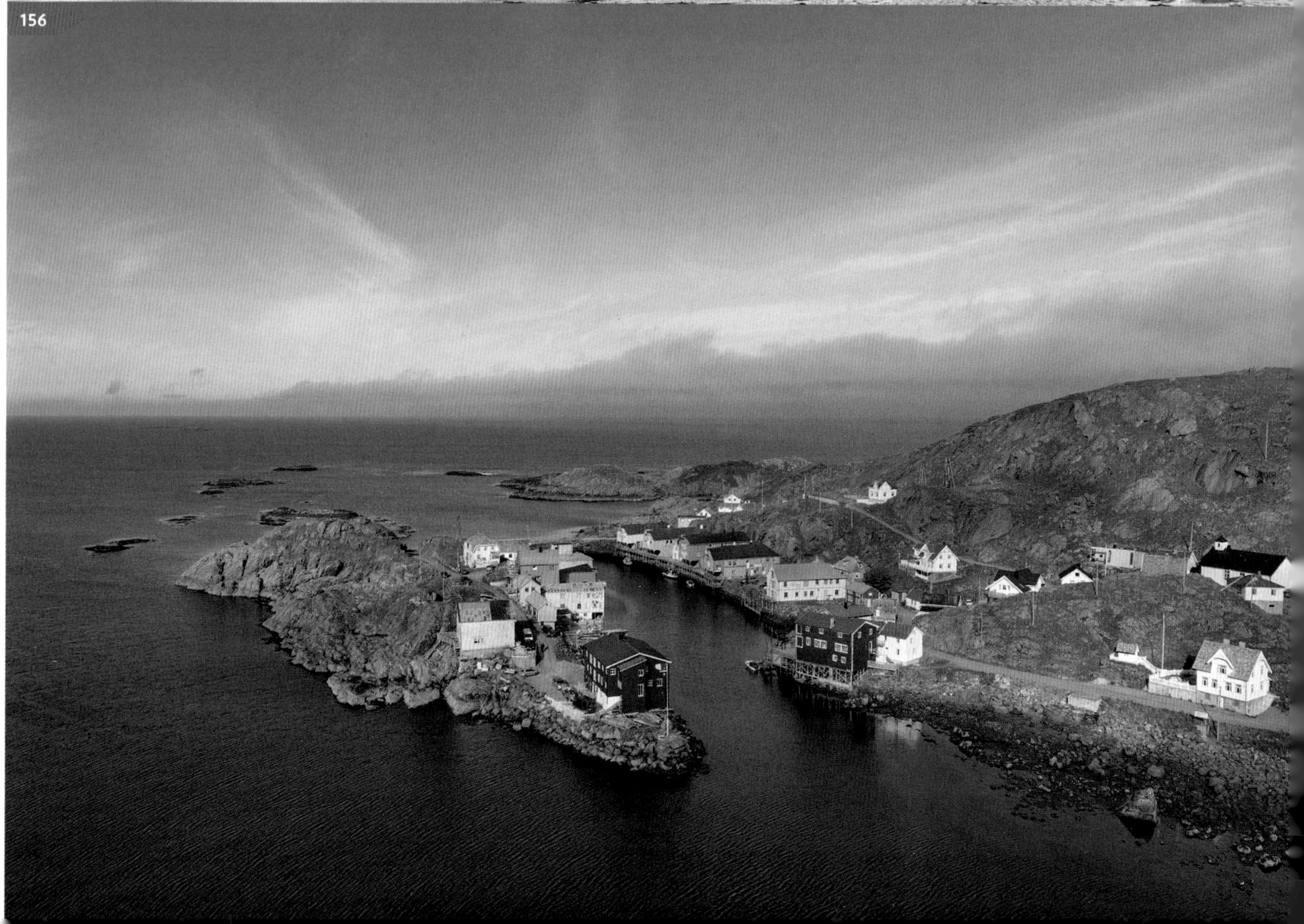

158

159

155 Norway's longest sandy beach at Bleik in Vesterålen.

156 A fishing village in Nordland.

157 You get a fantastic view towards the sea from Mount Aunfjell outside Harstad.

158 Go on a whale safari and experience sperm whales, which are fully protected in Norway.

159 The killer whale is losely related to the dolphins. It can be up to 10 metres long and weigh several tonnes.

160 With its approximately 70,000 inhabitants, Tromsø is Northern Norway's largest city and quite appropriately called the Paris of the North.

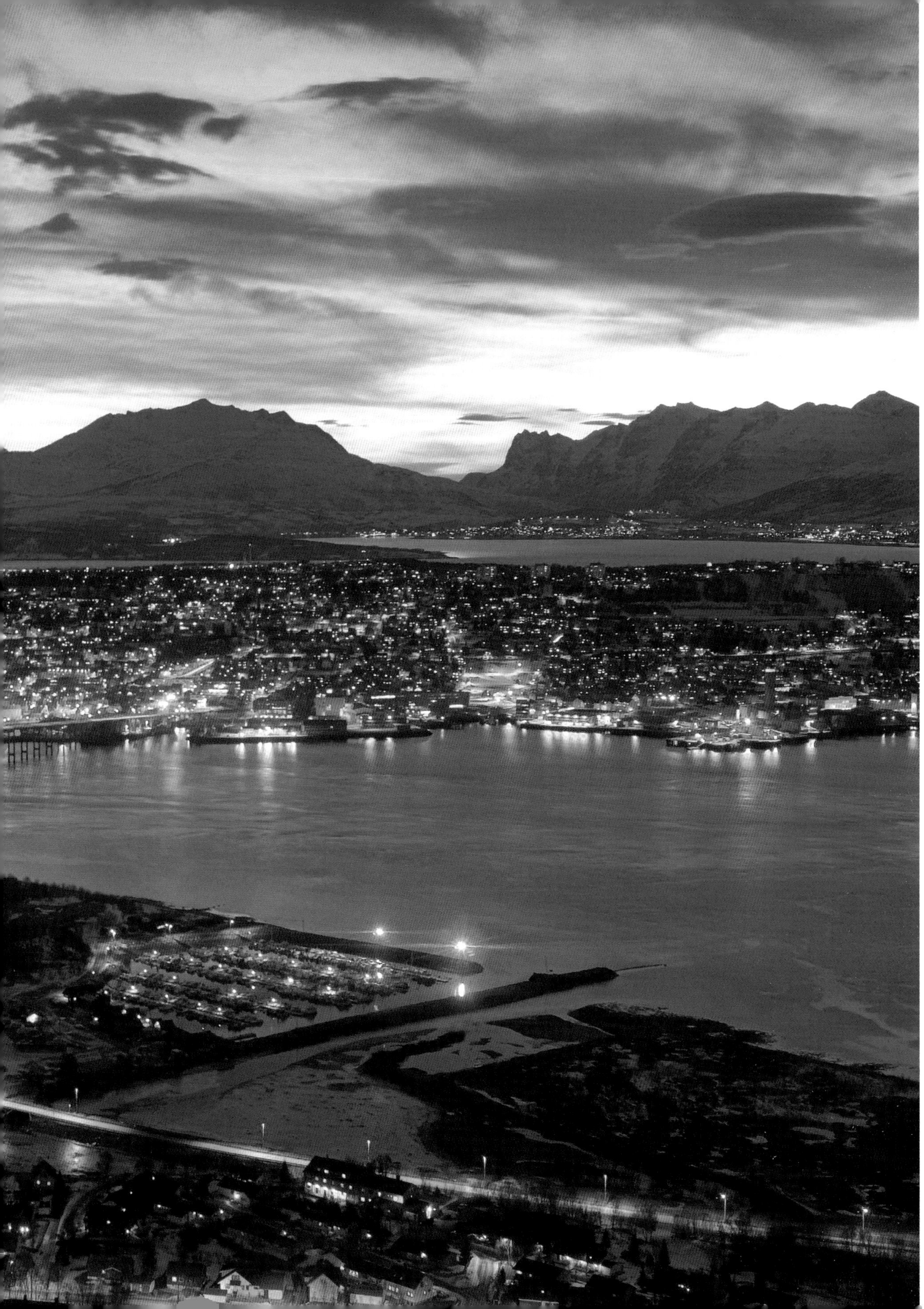

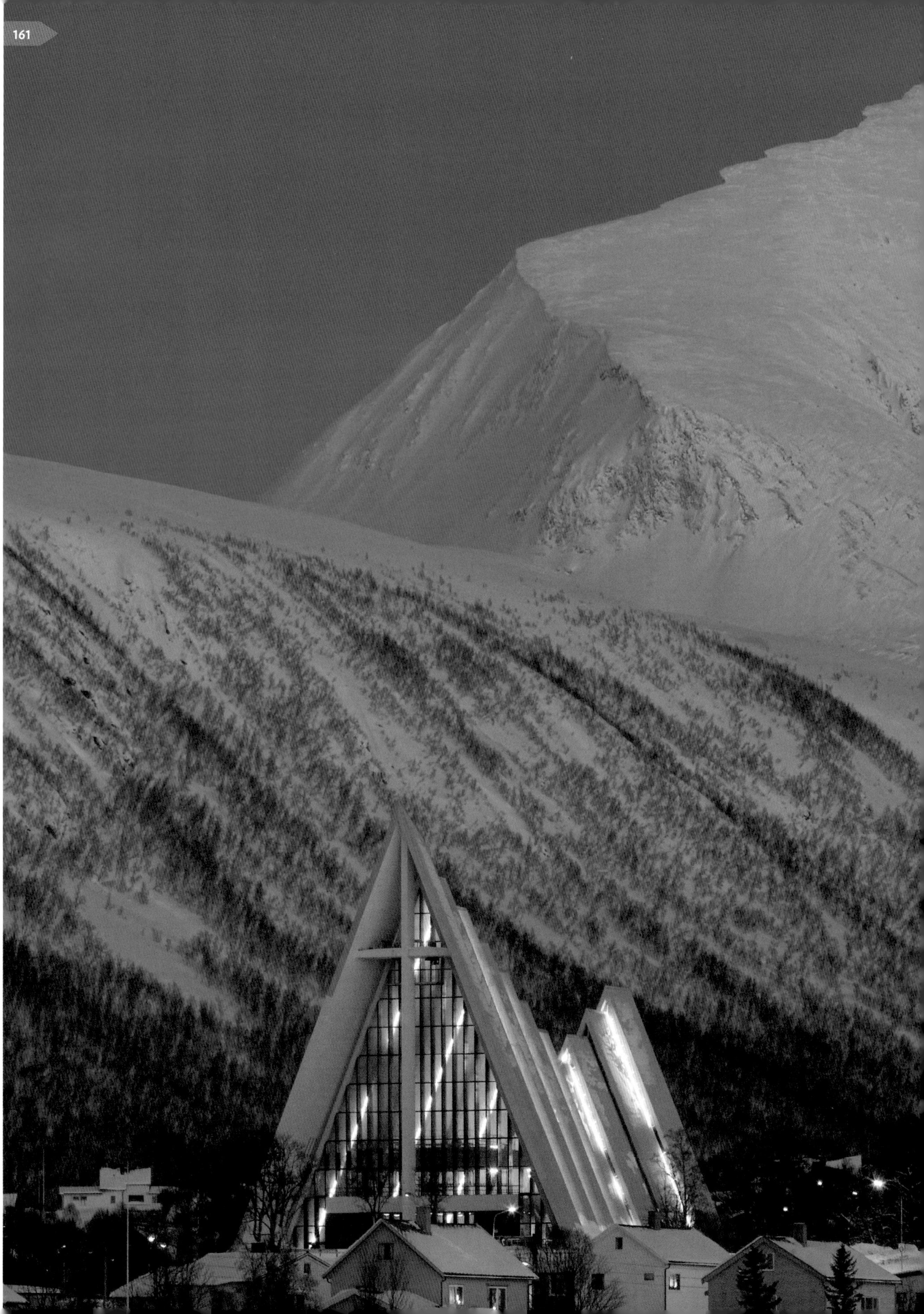

163

164

161 The Arctic Cathedral in Tromsø. The cathedral was completed
in 1965. The light-coloured sections, and even the shape of the
cathedral, make you associate it with an iceberg. The cathedral
is extremely visible in the landscape and is the city's greatest
landmark.

162 The magnificent view over Tromsø can be enjoyed by taking
the cable car from the city.

163 Dog sleighing at Tromsø Villmarksenter at Kvaløya, south of
Tromsø.

164 Sport fisherman in Reisa National Park.

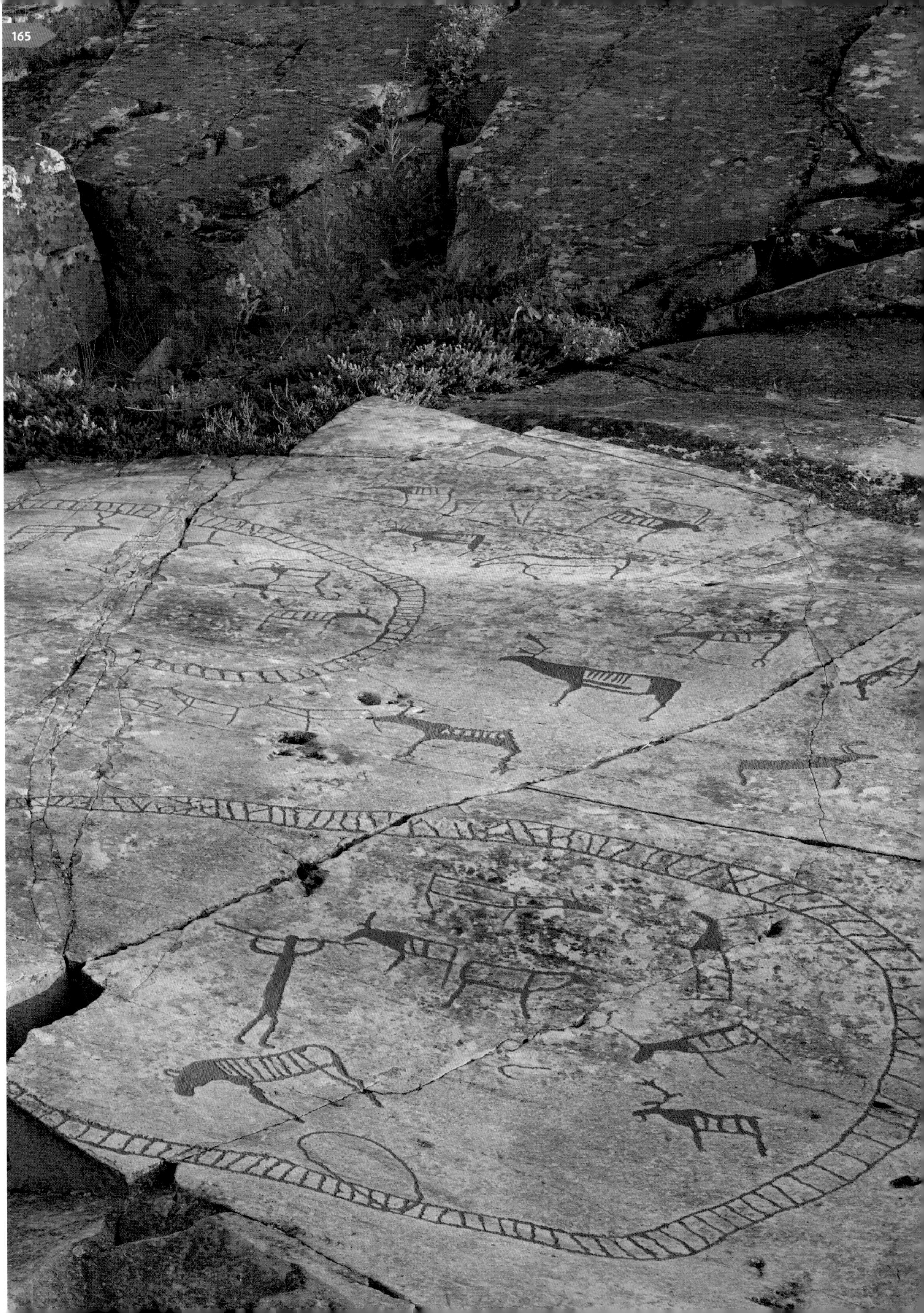

165 In Alta you will find Northern Europe's largest collection of petroglyphs, which are between 2500 and 6500 years old. Since 1973, 6000 of such rock carvings have been found in several places in Alta. The rock carvings have been included on UNESCO's World Culture and Natural Heritage List.

166 The Meridian Monument in Hammerfest stands on one of 34 sites in ten different countries, which form the Struve Meridian Arc. The monument was erected in 1854 to commemorate the largest international measuring of the shape and size of the earth. The Meridian Arc is included in UNESCO's World Heritage List.

167 The Ice Hotel in Alta is a hotel made of ice and snow. The inside temperature remains at minus 5 degrees Celsius throughout the winter. The hotel was first built in the year 2000, however since then it has been rebuilt every year.

169

170

168 Reindeer is a type of deer that lives in the north. It is crucial to the Sami people's livelihood. This is first and foremost due to its meat, skin and antlers. Every year flocks of reindeer must be moved from grazing pastures to grazing pastures, and these reindeer operations are linked to many Sami people's way of life and culture.

169 Reindeer and sleigh.

170 A Sami family with their characteristic traditional costumes.

171 The midnight sun at the North Cape.

172 The North Cape Plateau.

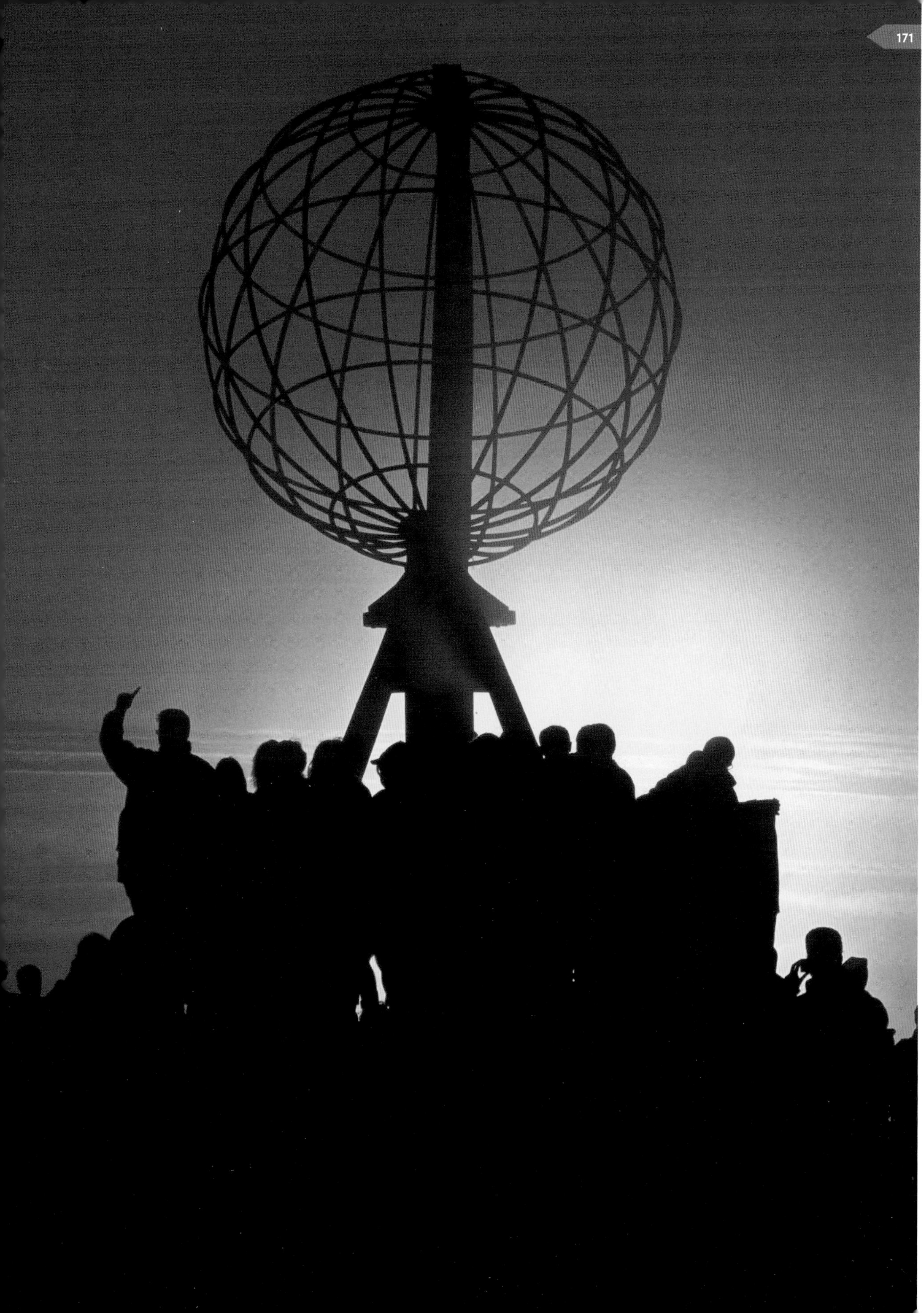

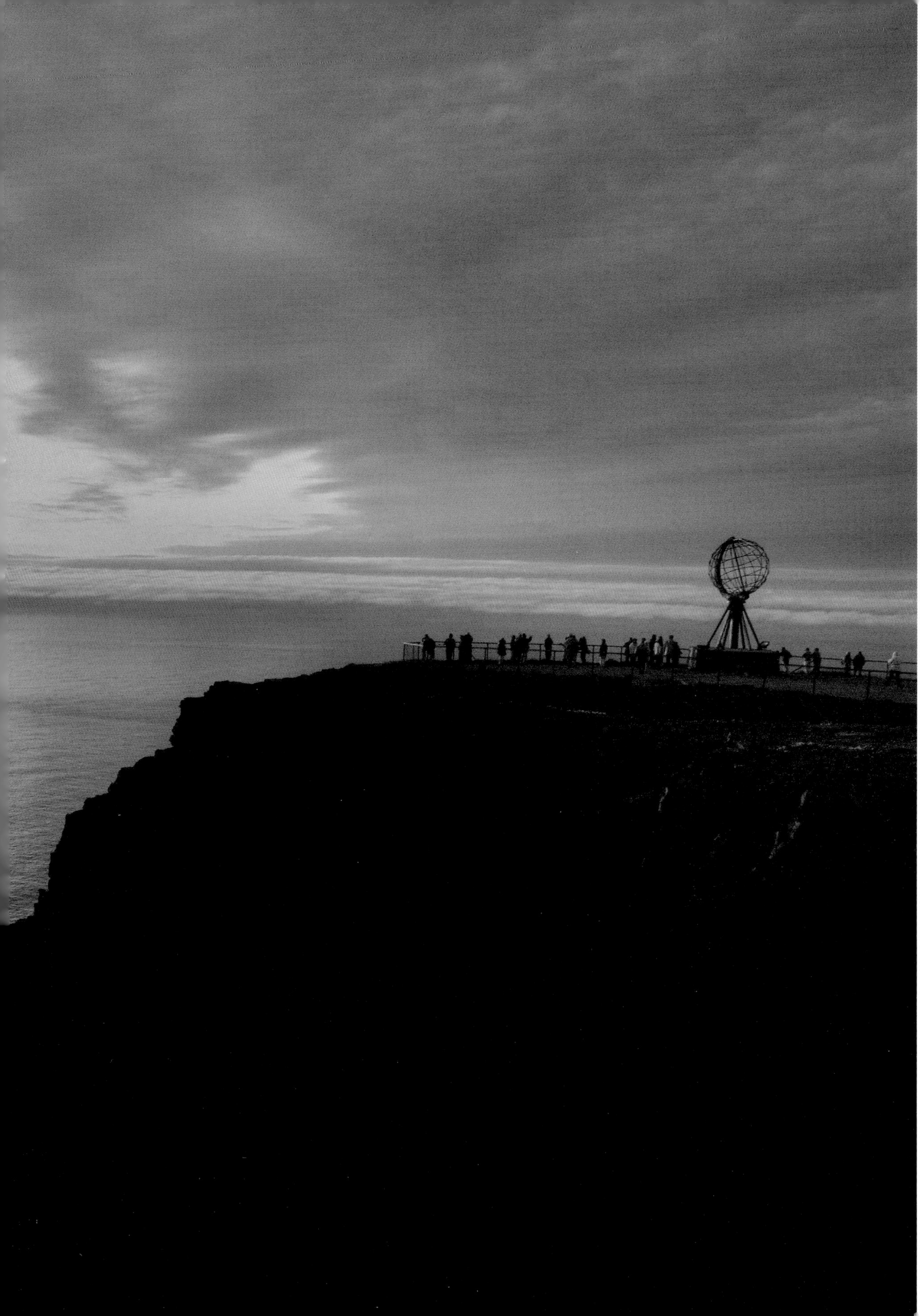

173

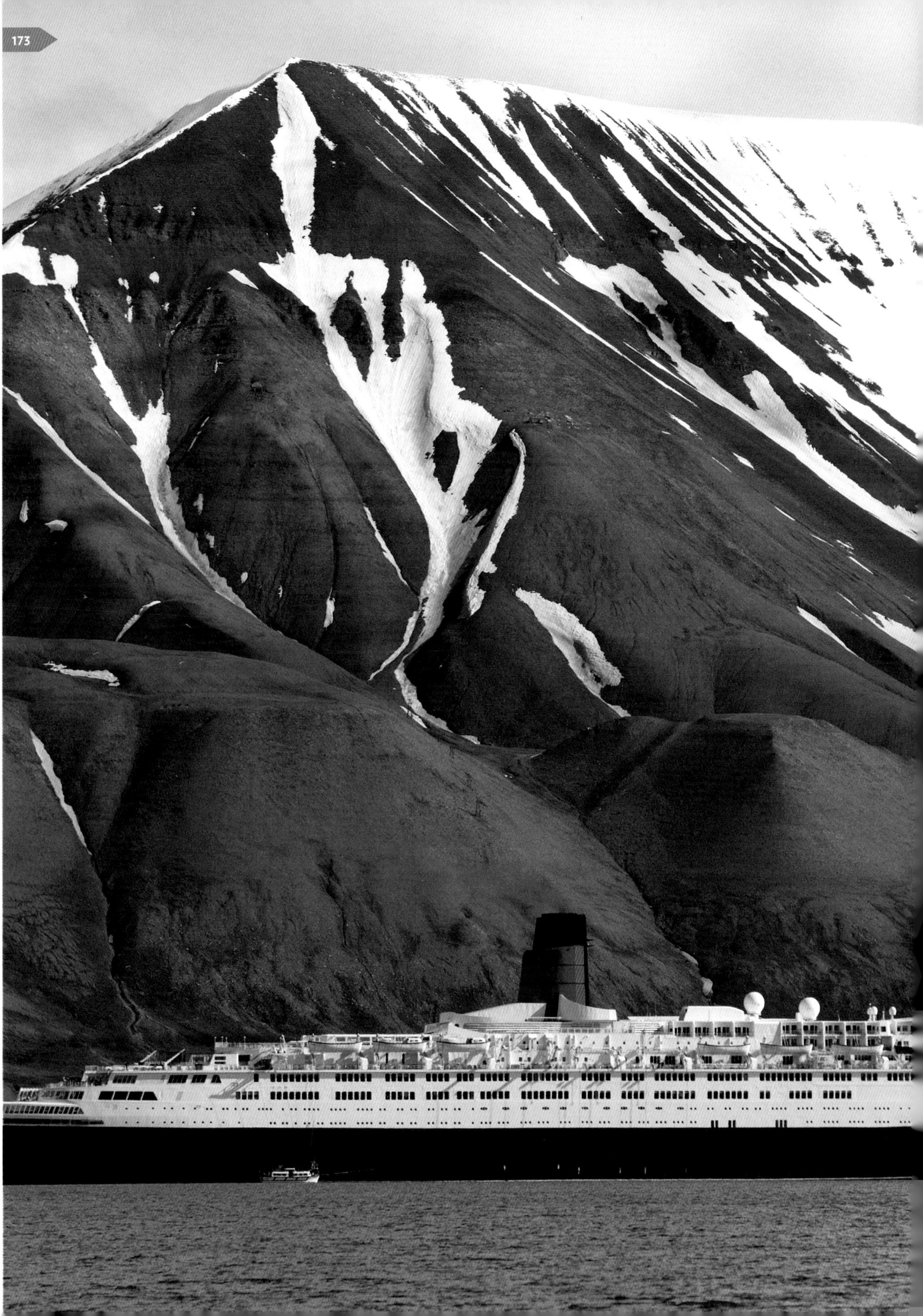

SVALBARD – HOME OF THE POLAR BEAR

During the summer, the Svalbard archipelago is bathed in a sun that never sets, while in the winter the northern lights cast their glow over the landscape. Svalbard is a very special part of Norway and one of the most northern areas of land in the world. Because Svalbard has an isolated location, the area has not been greatly affected by humans. Most of it remains untouched nature with no roads and other human intervention.

The Arctic Svalbard archipelago lies halfway between mainland Norway and the North Pole. The nature in Svalbard is characterised by enormous glaciers and wide mountain plateaus. However, despite the harsh Arctic climate, Svalbard has rich animal life with polar bears, walruses and a variety of other animals and bird species that have adapted to the cold climate. Substantial coal findings were fundamental to the mining communities in Longyearbyen and Barentsburg.

Svalbard was discovered in 1596. The islands were initially used by whale hunters as a catch base from the 1700s, however they were gradually abandoned. At the beginning of the 1800s coal mining operations were introduced, which led to the establishment of more communities. Today approximately 2600 inhabitants live on Svalbard, most of them in Longyearbyen.

The beautiful mountainous countryside is a world of adventure for geologists and tourists. More than half of Svalbards 63,000 square kilometres of surface area is covered by ice. The coastline has sharp mountains and Svalbard's largest island, Spitsbergen, is named after these.

Svalbard's fjords and glaciers can take your breath away in stunning nature that entices and frightens you simultaneously.

Experience the endlessness of the Arctic from a boat, by dog sleigh, on a snow scooter, hiking or on skis.

Arctic nature is unique, but extremely vulnerable. The rich animal and plant life are exposed to harsh conditions. Tourism is increasing a lot, however it is strictly regulated and all traffic and activity on Svalbard is based on the preservation of the environment.

As a guest, you also have a responsibility. Take good care of Svalbard!

173 Tourism in Svalbard has significantly increased. More and more people elect to take the excursion to Svalbard on a cruise ship, which allows you to experience the magnificent nature at close hand.

174 Snow scooters are a normal mode of transport on Svalbard, where snow is on the ground most of the year.

175 Polar bears on drift ice. Polar bears are, along with Kodiak bears, the largest bears and predators. They can weigh up to 800 kg.

176 Beautiful mountain formations along the west side of Svalbard under the midnight sun.

THE STORY OF THE TROLLS

When humans settled in Norway approximately ten thousand years ago, they soon discovered that the country was already inhabited. Some strange creatures had come before them. In hills and homesteads the pixies lived. In rivers and waterfalls lived the Fossegrimen spirit, and in black, bottomless small forest lakes ruled the Nixie. However, deep in the mountains the worst of them all lived – the nasty trolls.

The trolls looked like humans but they only had four fingers and four toes. They had long noses and cow-like tails. Some of the trolls were huge and preferably had tree and moss-like growths on their heads and growing out their noses. Others were tiny. Two-headed and three-headed trolls could also be seen, and some had only one eye on their foreheads. They all grew to be very old.

They could only be seen at night or at dusk, because trolls could not stand daylight. If they did not go into the mountains before dawn they exploded and turned into stones. Several turned-to-stone trolls can be seen around Norway, for example, Trolltindene in Romsdal and Svolværgeita in Lofoten.

The wrath of trolls knew no bounds. Therefore, it was important to have a peaceful relationship with them. Heaven forbid the farmer who declined to show the trolls respect! If this happened both he and his livestock could be subject to sickness and injury. Therefore, the farmer put out a very full dish of porridge for them every Christmas Eve, and the porridge was always eaten up.

The trolls were not only angry, but also very strong, and they could throw battle stones against churches or other things they did not like. In this way, the trolls left their mark in the terrain. These have been used as 'evidence' of their existence.

One of the greatest dangers of being exposed to a troll was being captured and taken to the rocks. Of those who were captured, some were only held in captivation for a few minutes or hours, while others never returned. The trolls were evil and dangerous, however humans discovered that they had a conciliatory trait: they were so witless that one could almost feel sorry for them.

In Henrik Ibsen's dramatic poem Peer Gynt from 1867, we meet the King of trolls, Dovregubben, who was actually not as witless as the other trolls. Today we know trolls best from stories, legends and folk songs, particularly from Asbjørnsen and Moe's Norwegian Folk Stories from 1844.

177 Trolls in Hunderfossen Family Park located in Gudbrandsdalen, north of Lillehammer.

178 The harmless trolls welcome you at the top of Mount Trollstigen.

179 A good-natured troll.

180 Trolls in Hunderfossen Family Park.

181 The mystical atmosphere that nature sometimes portrays has led to the belief that trolls really do exist.

182 Along the mountain road of Trollstigen, people have finally been given permission to put up a warning sign about trolls!

183 Wintermorning in mountain forest.

181

182

© CAPPELEN DAMM AS 2012

PICTURE EDITOR Bård Løken
DESIGN Laboremus Oslo [João Doria & Rune Døli]
PRINTING AND BINDING Livonia Print Sia, 2014, Latvia

ISBN 978-82-02-38153-0

Third printing, 2014

OTHER EDITIONS
Norwegian edition   ISBN 978-82-02-38000-7
German edition   ISBN 978-82-02-38155-4
French edition   ISBN 978-82-02-38154-7
Spanish edition   ISBN 978-82-02-38156-1
Italian edition   ISBN 978-82-02-38159-2
Dutch edition   ISBN 978-82-02-38161-5
Polish edition   ISBN 978-82-02-38158-5
Russian edition   ISBN 978-82-02-38157-8
Chinese edition   ISBN 978-82-02-38160-8

Cappelen Damm AS
N-0055 Oslo
www.cappelendamm.no

PICTURE CREDITS / FRONT COVER
Blossoming fruit trees, Hardanger © Stig Tronvold / NN / Samfoto
World Ski Championship, Holmenkollen 2011 © Erik Johansen /
Scanpix

PICTURE CREDITS / BACK COVER
iStockphoto

PICTURE CREDITS / CONTENTS

© Helge Sunde / Samfoto: 001
© Bård Løken / NN / Samfoto: 002, 004, 003, 013, 017, 024, 025, 026,
    035, 037, 038, 039, 041, 044, 045, 046, 051, 057, 058, 059, 064,
    065, 074, 075, 076, 083, 084, 087, 089, 090, 092, 095, 097, 098,
    100, 101, 102, 103, 104, 106, 107, 114, 115, 116, 120, 121, 123, 124,
    126, 127, 128, 129, 132, 134, 137, 138, 139, 140, 142, 144, 145, 148,
    150, 151, 156, 157, 160, 161, 162, 163, 164, 165, 166, 167, 169, 170,
    171, 172, 177, 178, 182, 183
© Heiko Junge / Scanpix: 005, 006
© Roger Hardy / Samfoto: 007
© Bjørn Jørgensen / NN / Samfoto: 008
© Munch-museet/Munch-Ellingsen gruppen/BONO 2012. Photo
    Jacques Lathion / The National Museum of Art, Architecture
    and Design: 009
© Tom Schandy / NN / Samfoto: 010, 015, 048, 066
© Göran Bohlin / VG: 011
© Espen Bratlie / Samfoto: 012, 018, 019, 029, 030, 031, 052, 060, 063,
    109, 155
© Øystein Søbye / NN / Samfoto: 014, 033, 034, 036
© Jens Sølvberg / Samfoto: 016
© Vigeland-museet. Photo Svein Grønvold / NN / Samfoto: 020
© Vigeland-museet. Photo Kerstin Mertens / Samfoto: 021
© Vigeland-museet. Photo Bård Løken / NN / Samfoto: 022, 023
© Håkon Fagerås. Photo Bård Løken / NN / Samfoto: 027
© Jan Petter Lynau / VG: 028
© Thorfinn Bekkelund / Samfoto: 032, 122
© Helge Sunde / Samfoto: 040, 042, 079, 080, 081, 091, 149
© Svein Erik Dahl / Samfoto: 045
© Stig Børre Elvegård / NN / Samfoto: 047
© Tore Wuttudal / NN / Samfoto: 049, 053, 133, 154, 175, 180
© Steinar Myhr / NN / Samfoto: 050, 069, 105, 130, 131
© Ove Bergersen / NN / Samfoto: 054, 061, 118, 176
© Svein Grønvold / NN / Samfoto: 055, 158,
© Sigmund Krøvel-Velle / Samfoto: 056, 147
© Fred Friberg / NN / Samfoto: 062
© Kjell-Erik Moseid / NN / Samfoto: 067, 073, 108
© Willy Haraldsen /Scanpix: 068
© Fritz Røed/BONO 2012. Photo Bård Løken / NN / Samfoto: 070
© Johannes Haugan / NN / Samfoto: 071
© Baard Næss / NN / Samfoto: 072, 110
© Odd Mehus / Aftenposten: 082
© Stig Tronvold / NN / Samfoto: 085, 094, 099
© Pål Hermansen: 086, 168
© Per Eide / Samfoto: 087, 117
© Jan Rabben / Samfoto: 088
© Sara Johannessen / VG: 097
© Arne Aasheim: 111
© Jarle Wæhler / Statens Vegvesen: 112
© Henrik Trygg / Corbis: 113
© Terje Rakke / Nordic Life: 121
© Thorfinn Bekkelund / Samfoto: 125
© Erlend Haarberg / NN / Samfoto: 135, 136
© Dag G. Nordsveen / Samfoto: 141
© Bjørn Jørgensen / NN / Samfoto: 143
© Kai Jensen / Scanpix: 146, 173
© Trym Ivar Bergsmo / Samfoto: 152, 153
© Pål Hermansen / NN / Samfoto: 159
© Fredrik Naumann / Samfoto: 174
© trollsofnorway.com: 179
© Dag Jensen / Samfoto: 181
© iStockphoto: 077, 078, 095, 096, 119, front/end papers